MURDER AND MAYHEM

The Anthology of American Serial Killers

From the 19th and Early 20th Centuries

MURDER AND MAYHEM

The Anthology of American
Serial Killers

From the 19th and Early 20th Centuries

Edited with an Introduction by
Taylar Banks

WHITLOCK PUBLISHING
Alfred, New York

First Whitlock Publishing edition 2019

Whitlock Publishing
Alfred, New York
http://www.whitlockpublishing.com

Editorial matter @ Taylar Banks

ISBN: 978-1-943115-30-3

This book was set in Adobe Garamond Pro on 50# acid-free paper
that meets ANSI standards for archival quality.

ACKNOWLEDGMENTS

I would like to thank my best friend Kristyn for pushing and motivating me through the entire process of this book, my mom for always supporting me, Dr. Grove for giving me the opportunity to create it, Haley Ruffner for being such a big help, and Jared Cooper for always believing I would be published. Thank you to my family and friends as well for all of your support.

TABLE OF CONTENTS

INTRODUCTION

"Serial killers appeal to the most basic and powerful instinct in all of us—that is, survival. The total disregard for life and the suffering of others exhibited by serial killers shocks our sense of humanity and makes us question our safety and security."

-Scott A. Bonn Ph.D., Psychology

HERE LIES AN ANTHOLOGY about some of the most prolific American serial killers of the 19th and early 20th centuries. This book contains four known serial killers and one serial killing "family." This includes the notorious H. H. Holmes; Jesse Harding Pomeroy, one of the youngest known serial killers; the mysterious family, the Bloody Benders; Lydia Sherman "The Derby Poisoner" who killed six of her children; and Belle Gunness who used her farm as a burial site for her victims.

You will read about each of their methodologies. Some include torture, bludgeoning, mutilation, asphyxiation, and poison; some are written with precise detail. Some of their methods will make your skin crawl such as H. H. Holmes' murder castle with stairs that led to nowhere, and Jesse Harding Pomeroy's desire to torture and kill children.

In the early 20th century, awareness of serial crime was limited, and the phenomena was new to investigators. The technology and knowledge needed to effectively convict criminals didn't yet exist.

A viewpoint from the 19th and early 20th centuries was that killers were monsters, part of a supernatural world, or possessed by an evil force. The criminals were viewed as "destructive, [a] self-perpetuating class, homeless and rootless, urban-based, immigrant, intemperate, and ill-educated," according to Harvey J. Graff, an Ohio Eminent Scholar in Literacy Studies and Professor of English and History at The Ohio State University, in his essay, "Crime and Punishment in the Nineteenth Century: A New Look at the Criminal." He discusses criminals and patterns of crime in the nineteenth and early twentieth centuries. He mentions how criminals are exploited and examines crime and history. Murderers have always been subject to these stereotypes. However, not all of them are ill-educated, and they are typically not homeless. For example, H. H. Holmes was a businessman and a doctor who had money. Jane Toppan was a nurse. The Zodiac Killer was intelligent enough to never be caught. Some stereotypes have changed, such as many believing they are homeless and rootless. However, there are still many faulty stereotypes that continue to be passed on as being true.

In 2008, Robert J. Morton, supervisory special agent, and Mark A. Hilts, the unit chief of the FBI behavioral unit, mentioned myths about serial killers in their book, *Serial Murder Pathways to Investigation*. Movies, books, and television have represented serial murders.

A common myth is that all serial killers are white males. However, Clementine Barnabet was an African American female serial killer who joined a cult called the Church of Sacrifice. This put her on a path of crime; she confessed to 35 murders. Coral Eugene Watts, also known as the "Sunday Morning Slasher," was a black man who murdered approximately seventeen women.

In TV shows such as *Dexter*, who is a white male serial killer who kills other criminals, most are white males. This gives the idea that there are few minority serial killers. Some researchers think it is a lack of acknowledging crime amongst other races and minority groups. The idea is the media is so used to focusing on white males that they don't branch out into other groups of people. This is a dangerous image of serial killers because it neglects to inform people that a serial killer could be anyone.

Another common stereotype is that serial killers can't maintain long-term relationships, and they're misfits. This is inaccurate.

Herbert Richard Baumeister, a suspected serial killer who murdered over a dozen men, was married for 23 years and had three children. *People Magazine* said, "For Julie Baumeister the shock was all the more jarring because of the close-knit, even cloistered, family life she and Herb had tried to build at Fox Hollow Farm. The Baumeister's, who had few friends, showered their attention on their children." Julie said Herb was a "dedicated parent." He helped choose his children's preschool, made sure they had Christmas presents, and made them lunch.

John Wayne Gacy, "The Killer Clown," was not a misfit. He had a wife, a son, and a daughter. Gacy's father abused and degraded him as a child. However, in school, Gacy used to volunteer to run errands for teachers and neighbors. He did not end up finishing high school but went to Northwestern Business College and graduated in 1963. Gacy pushed himself to prove to his father and to himself that he was not worthless. He was also charitable at fundraising events and parades. At children's parties, he dressed as a character he created, "Pogo the Clown." In addition, he managed three KFC restaurants in Waterloo, Iowa, and joined the local United States Junior Chamber called Jaycees, a leadership and civic organization that emphasized business development, management skills, and community service. Gacy was later appointed to the Boards of Directors for Jaycees. However, Jaycees had a hidden dark side that involved wife swapping, prostitution, pornography, and drug use which Gacy participated in. Nevertheless, he stayed active in his community.

Many serial killers are capable of living what seem to be normal lives, but they have a dark side. People are interested in the unusual and what's not socially acceptable. Murder sparks an uneasy feeling about human capability. There are investigation shows that examine serial killers; for example, the American crime show *Criminal Minds* explores serial killer's character and gets inside of their minds to understand who they are, why they're killing, and how to capture them. People often want to understand how and why serial killers do what they do. For example, Lydia Sherman killed her three husbands and children without any clear reason for doing so. People are interested in understandng how a person can have a total disregard for the life of others. It keeps them on their toes and gives them chills to see something so unnatural, inhumane, and brutal. This attitude draws people in.

Scott Boon, a criminologist and professor at Drew University, in a nutshell says, people are attracted to tragedy and the horrors of the world. They see disaster and have overwhelming emotions because terrible things happen. He adds that we're able to experience horror and fear in a comfortable and controlled environment. There's excitement, but there's no threat and that's the thrill. "The public is drawn to true crime because it triggers the most basic and powerful emotion in all of us—fear."

Lydia Sherman
"The Derby Poisoner"

(December 24, 1824-May 16, 1878)

SHE WAS AN AMERICAN SERIAL KILLER who poisoned six of her children along with two other children. She also killed three of her husbands and was convicted of second-degree murder.

Lydia Sherman was born in Burlington, New Jersey. When she was less than a year old, her mother died, and her father became a butcher in Trenton. Her father remarried; Lydia didn't like her stepmother and went to live with her aunt in New Brunswick. She lived there until she was 17 years old and met Edward Struck, a police officer in an upper ward of New York City. Struck himself had been married before and had two children. Edward and Lydia lived together for seven years and had six children.

In the early 1860s, Edward fell ill and suddenly died. The physician who examined the body said he didn't know what Struck had died from. However, friends, family, and neighbors said the symptoms he showed were that of being poisoned. Lydia claimed her husband had taken the wrong medicine. After the death of her husband, Lydia's six children all died in the span of two years; she poisoned them. Oddly enough, there were no suspicions at the time. She went on to marry two more times killing both men, a step son, and a step daughter.

A doctor later examined the bodies and discovered Lydia had killed her husband and children, so she fled to New York. However, she was captured in 1872 and charged with second-degree murder and faced life in prison. After five years into her sentence, she escaped using the excuse of being sick and got a job as a housekeeper for a rich widower in Providence. She was caught and sent back to prison. On May 16, 1878, Lydia died of cancer at Wethersfield State Prison in Connecticut.

TIMELINE

1824   -On December 24, Lydia Sherman is born

1860s   -She marries a policeman, Edward Struck
        -Edward and Lydia have six children
        -Lydia purchases rat poison and kills her husband
        -She poisons her six children

1868   -Lydia marries Dennis Hurlburt

1870   -Lydia is a widow again
        -In April, she becomes a housekeeper for Nelson Sherman
        -Lydia poisons and kills Nelson's son and daughter
        with arsenic

1871   -On May 12, Lydia poisons Dennis and he dies
        -Dr Beardsly, the local doctor, is skeptical about the deaths
        and discovers the children and husbands were poisoned
        -Lydia flees to New York

1872   -Lydia is captured and charged with second-degree
        murder and faces life imprisonment

1878   -On May 16, Lydia dies of cancer in Wethersfield
        State Prison

THE POISON FIEND!

LIFE, CRIMES AND CONVICTION

OF

LYDIA SHERMAN,

(THE MODERN LUCRETIA BORGIA,)

RECENTLY TRIED IN NEW HAVEN, CONN., FOR

POISONING

THREE HUSBANDS AND EIGHT OF HER CHILDREN

HER LIFE IN FULL!

EXCITING ACCOUNT OF HER TRIAL-THE FEARFUL EVIDENCE

MOST STARTLING AND SENSATIONAL SERIES OF CRIMES
EVER COMMITTED IN THIS COUNTRY.

HER CONVICTION

AND

CONFESSION.

PHILADELPHIA:
BARCLAY & CO., PUBLISHERS,
21 N. SEVENTH STREET.
1873.

Lydia Sherman, her maiden name Danbury, is a native of Burlington, NJ. When she was less than a year old, her mother died, and her father became a butcher at Trenton. She lived under the paternal roof until her father remarried. Not liking her stepmother, she went to live with her aunt at New Brunswick. Here she remained until seventeen years old, when she became acquainted with Edward Struck, a police officer in one of the upper wards of New York City, to whom she was married. Struck had been married before and had two children who were now placed under guardians. The newly married couple lived together nearly seven years, during which time six children were born. And now begins the awful events which throw such an air of mystery around the woman accused of eleven murders. First, her husband was taken sick and suddenly died. It appears that a physician attended, who said he didn't know what the man died of. The symptoms, as described by those who saw him, were those of a person who had taken poison. Mrs. Sherman said the cause of his death was his getting up in the absence of the doctor and taking the wrong medicine. Subsequent to the death of her husband, her children all died in a span of about two years, and no one seemed to know what ailed them, except this—they all died suddenly.

Mrs. Sherman—or Mrs. Struck, as she was then named—spent two years after the death of her first husband as a seamstress and nurse. She next got employment in a sewing machine store om Canal Street, where she made the acquaintance of a Mr. Curtis, who afterward engaged her to live with his mother at Stratford, about nine miles from this place. It was while living there that she became acquainted with her second husband, a man named Hurlbut, who lived at Huntington, and who was thought to be quite well off. At his death he left considerable real estate, beside $10,000 in cash. This man had lived quietly and economically as a farmer and fisherman and was well known to all around by the name "Old Hurlbut." Mrs. Sherman professed a great fondness for her husband, and it was not long before he made a will bequeathing all his property to her in the event of his death. They lived on apparently happy, the neighbors noticing that every time he returned from his business, she met him at the door and kissed him. Time passed on, and one day Dr. Church, the village physician, was summoned to attend Mr. Hurlbut. On arriving at the house, he found him suffering acute pains in the head and stomach, accompanied by an intense burning, as if the patient had a violent fever. Dr. Church, becoming alarmed at the critical condition of his patient, sent for consulting physicians. "Old Hurlbut" died before the doctors had agreed upon a diagnosis and was buried out of sight.

Nelson H. Sherman was a skilled mechanic and a man much loved for his genial spirits. Indeed, his greatest fault was too much generosity. A little more than a year and a half ago [1]his wife died, leaving him with four children, the eldest, a son named Nelson, aged seventeen; a daughter Addie, aged fourteen; another boy, Nattie, aged four years, and an infant five months old. Nelson H. Sherman first became acquainted with Lydia, the widow Hurlbut, at her residence near the river in Derby, CT., and after a short courtship was married to her in September 1870. They settled in the house where Sherman and his children died. From that stage on to the present time, the facts relating to the career of this mysterious woman are clearer and more terrible in proportion. The next person to become "suddenly ill" was Mr. Sherman's infant by his former wife, which died in a few days. The next victim, either to the devilish designs of the prisoner or to the strangest series of fatalities on record, was the much-loved daughter of Mr. Sherman. Her father, as soon as he found her symptoms were dangerous, became greatly alarmed, and summoned the advice of several physicians. The symptoms in all these cases appeared to be the same — that of acute pains in the head and stomach, with intense fever. The doctors found it impossible to help the girl, and in a few days, she was lying in the grave beside her infant sister.

It now transpires that Sherman and his wife, though but recently married, had already had secret troubles of a very serious nature, and though living in the same house, did not cohabit. Mr. Sherman had for some time slept with the baby, and Mrs. Sherman had slept alone. On the 11th of May, Sherman started

1. Roughly 1869

off with several friends in New Haven, telling his wife he would be back that night. It appears that the party all got to drinking. Sherman, among the rest, did not return for about a week. When they proposed to go back, Sherman objected to going at all, and so the rest of the party went by the cars, leaving Sherman with the team[2] in the city. Young Nelson, after waiting a day or two longer, said he was going to find his father. Mrs. Sherman gave him $2.50, and he went in search. Sherman was found in a den with low people. The father and boy returned together. Sherman was in a very bad way and unable to go to work for several days. Finally, when he did go to the factory, he appeared very low spirited and would not go home to his meals. Mrs. Sherman here appeared to have considerable regard for him, for each day she sent his meals to him, the best she could get. About this time, Mrs. Sherman remonstrated with her husband for refusing to cohabit, saying it was wrong. He replied that "he knew too much of her, and that he should soon begin to talk out to her." He also told her that many of the neighbors knew as much as he did, and that there would soon be trouble. Mrs. Sherman was still doctoring her husband for his sickness, mixing up various kinds of potions, which he drank. Each time that he came into the house she greeted him with a kiss.

About the 1st of June, Sherman, after drinking his usual evening beverage mixed by his wife, went downtown. Two hours after he came back, he sat down on a chair and said he had a bad headache. The headache was followed by a raging fever and fearful cramps in the stomach. doctors Kinney and Beardsley both attended him, but he died after two days, suffering dreadful agonies. The doctors held another consultation after his death, and, as the symptoms of the sick man had been precisely those of his two daughters, they decided to hold a post-mortem examination. Accordingly, the stomach was taken out, besides about is a third part of the liver. These were boxed up and sent to Professor Barker at New Haven for analysis. It required nearly three weeks to make the analysis, and it is only a short time since that <u>the startling re</u>port of the proof went in, saying the liver had

2. Typically two horses pulling a carriage or wagon

been found perfectly saturated with arsenic, and that there was enough in it to kill three men. A warrant was at once sued out for Mrs. Sherman's arrest and put in the hands of Deputy Sheriff Henry A. Blakeman for execution at the proper time. Since the suspicion had grown so strong, young Nelson, his brother Nattie, and their grandmother, had all left the house, through fear that they might become the next victims if they stayed. Mrs. Sherman was not arrested immediately, but she was closely watched by the sheriff and the men employed by him. Although the report of the chemist had been kept as secret as possible, its import had become known and was discussed on the public street. In two or three days, Mrs. Sherman, not knowing that she was watched, quietly moved to New Brunswick, NJ., where the police had the woman under surveillance for two or three weeks, awaiting the collection of sufficient evidence to warrant her arrest and to enable the officers to secure a requisition from Gov. Jewell. Not long after, Deputy Sheriff Blakeman of New Haven, CT., arrived at New Brunswick and communicated all his facts to Chief of Police Oliver. The woman had gone to New York, where she was being shadowed by a detective, and the officers awaited her return at the depot for several hours. She came on the 10:50 train, with a companion, and was immediately arrested.

Immediately after she had left Derby, and succeeding the death of the child, the friends of Mr. Sherman took steps to investigate the matter, and to that end had the body of Mr. Sherman and those of the two children exhumed. The officers who came to make the arrest state that undeniable evidence of poison was found upon all three of the bodies, and that it was plainly seen in the stomach of the last buried of the three. They also state that they have been able to fix upon the alleged murderer the purchase of poison like that of which traces were found. That poison was a vegetable and of an unusual character, the officers being unable to give its name. They were not -to be communicative; but the above facts were elicited. They were armed with warrants and a requisition from Gov. Jewell. After the arrest, Chief Oliver and Detective Mitchell conveyed the woman to the office of District Attorney Herbert, where she was detained until four o'clock, at which time she was taken to New Haven, accompanied by Sheriff Blakeman and Detective Mitchell. The statements of the officers leave no doubt that the woman is guilty of one of the most startling and sensational series of crimes that has ever been committed in this part of the country.

"OLD HURLBUT," LYDIA SHERMAN'S SECOND HUSBAND, GROWS ILL, AS DID HIS POISONED PREDECESSOR, AND DYING LEAVES HER A WEALTHY WIDOW

THE TRIAL OF LYDIA SHERMAN

Her preliminary examination, before Justice Piatt, was held at Birmingham on the 6th and 7th July last; she was examined upon the charge of murdering her husband.

Frank, the youngest child of Mr. Sherman, was taken sick in December, and after a few days illness, while under the care of his stepmother and of his grandmother, Mrs. Jones, died with all the symptoms of arsenic poison.

A few weeks later another child, Addie, a beautiful girl, aged fifteen and a universal favorite in the village, was taken sick and died on New Year's Eve. She too showed symptoms of poison. In the May following, Sherman, who was a dissipated man, was taken ill and died, with symptoms of arsenic poison, on the 12th of that month. The evidence of Dr. Ambrose Beardsley, the Health Officer of the town and the physician who attended Sherman and his two children, showed that they had died of arsenic poison.

After Sherman's death, Lydia left for New Jersey, ostensibly on a visit Dr. Beardsley's suspicions having been aroused, he communicated with Dr. Kinney, a post-mortem examination was had upon Sherman, and later the graves of the children were opened, the contents of the stomachs secured and sent to New Haven for analysis.

The parties who had taken these preliminary proceedings acted very secretly, and on receiving the report of the chemises that sufficient arsenic was found in the stomach of each victim to cause death, they instituted inquiries into the antecedents of Mrs. Sherman, when the facts of her marriage to Dennis Hurlbut, a wealthy farmer, living in an adjoining town, and his mysterious death were ascertained. One very strong circumstance regarding Hurlbut's taking off was that the only person who was an occupant of the house with him during his illness was his wife, the accused. His grave was opened, the stomach secured and sent to New Haven for analysis. Unmistakable evidence of poison was found in its contents. Having carefully woven the web of circumstantial evidence around the accused, Dr. Beardsley and his associates communicated their investigations to A. H. Gilbert, the local Grand Juror, who went before Judge Pratt and secured a warrant for the arrest of the female Borgia. This was placed in the hands of Sheriff Henry A. Blakeman, who proceeded to New Jersey and arresting her, conveyed her to Birmingham, where the preliminary investigation already referred to was had. Colonel William B. Wooster and E. K. Foster, State Prosecuting Attorney, appearing for the people, and George B. Waterous of New Haven, and S. M. Gardener of Derby, for the defence. After a three-days patient hearing, she was committed to the county jail of New Haven on the charge of poisoning her husband.

This is considered one of the weakest cases of all the alleged murders committed by her in this state. The evidence heretofore given shows that she could have no incentive to the murder of Sherman unless to rid herself of a worthless husband who had no property of his own, and upon whom she had squandered several thousand dollars inherited from Hurlbut, that she might marry a more wealthy one. In the death of the children, she could not achieve any gain; in the death of her previous husband, Hurlbut, there was an incentive to the commission of the foul deed of which she is suspected. He was wealthy and had made his will, bequeathing at his effects to her. He was taken suddenly sick at his farmhouse; a neighbor passing was called in and requested to summon a physician. Dr. Shelton was called, prescribed, and Hurlbut died three days after, and was laid away in his last sleep, no one being in the house who could administer poison but the accused who attended him in his illness. Yet, Professor George F. Barker, who made the analysis of the stomach, swears that Dennis Hurlbut died from arsenic poison. If acquitted on the charge of poisoning Sherman, she will probably be placed on trial for poisoning the children, Frank and Addie. These three are the only murders charged against her in this county. In the event of her acquittal, she will no doubt be handed over to the authorities of Fairfield County to answer the charge of poisoning her second husband, Dennis Hurlbut, the evidence in which case is very explicit, and by all who are familiar with the facts is believed to be sufficient to convict her of the grave suspicions entertained that she killed Hurlbut for his property.

While these investigations were progressing, the authorities instituted inquiries into her antecedents in New York when it was discovered that she probably poisoned her first husband, Edward Struck, and five children, some of whom were her own offspring by him.

After Struck died, the next member of the family that "shuffled off the mortal "coil" was Edward Struck, Jr., aged about four years, who followed his father on July 5th, 1864, to Trinity Cemetery, and the same day his little sister Martha died, aged six years and nine months. The next to find a resting place in Trinity was William Struck, aged nine months and fifteen days. Then, on the 9th of March 1866, Ann Eliza Struck, aged twelve years, died, and was laid away to rest in the family plot. But death did not stop here. On May 19th, 1866, Lydia Struck[3], an accomplished young lady, aged eighteen years, eight months and eleven days, breathed her last breath the family residence.

Rev. Mr. Payson, of the Harlem Presbyterian Church, was present at the bedside of Lydia Struck when she died, and he describes the symptoms attending her illness as those of poisoning and recounted some months ago very suspicious circumstances against the accused.

It is said that Cornelius Struck, a conductor on the Third Avenue Railroad, and son of the deceased Struck, asked District Attorney Garvin to cause the bodies of his family to be exhumed and an analysis made of the stomachs. The motive that prompted this remarkable woman to administer poison to her victim, cannot, except in the case of Hurlbut, be divined. There is ground for grave suspicions that she may be responsible for more deaths; she was for some time employed as a nurse by Dr. L. Rodenstein in his practice in the upper part of the city and may have been administering deathly draughts to some of his patients. The indictment upon which she was arraigned was found on the 21st of September. It charges that, at the town of Derby, on the 8th of

3. Edward and Lydia's daughter

May 1871, Lydia Sherman, wife of Nelson H. Sherman, late of said place, did feloniously, willfully, etc., mix and mingle a great quantity of deadly poison called white arsenic, with a quantity of chocolate, which she administered to the said Sherman, who died on the 12th of May, and that the said Lydia Sherman is guilty of murder in the first degree. The second charge is the administration of poison in certain.

FIRST DAY OF TRIAL.

Lydia Sherman was placed on trial Tuesday, April 16th. She appeared unusually cheerful; she was dressed in a neat black alpaca dress, trimmed with silk velvet, a mixed black and white woolen shawl, white straw hat trimmed with black velvet and brown plume, from which drooped over her face a thin lace veil, through which her features were plainly marked, and upon her hands were black kid gloves. After the empaneling of the jury, she left the prisoner's box and took her seat beside her counsel, Messrs. Waterous, of this city, and S. M. Gardener, of Derby.

A little before eleven o'clock, Judge Sandford again took his seat on the bench and was accompanied by Justice Park of the Supreme Court, who was associated with him in the trial, the law requiring one of the Supreme Court Justices to be present. There appeared as counsel for the State, B. K. Foster, Col. William B. Wooster, and Col. Torrance, of Derby, and for the accused, Mr. George B. Waterous of New Haven, and Samuel M. Gardener of Derby.

At eleven o'clock Mr. Foster, the State Attorney, arose and said: "The grand jury have indicted Lydia Sherman for the murder of Nelson H. Sherman, and I move the Court that she be put on trial."

Mr. Wooster. — Has the prisoner been put to plea?

Mr. Foster. — She has not, I think.

The prisoner then arose, and the clerk commenced to read the indict merit. As the reading commenced, Mr. Waterous said: "Is it necessary that she should stand? The indictment is rather long."

The Court said that it was not, and Mr. Waterous then walked over to the prisoner and informed her that she might sit, but she smilingly declined, and said she would remain standing. The reading proceeded and the prisoner observed it carefully but with perfect calmness.

The clerk then said: "To this indictment what is your plea, guilty or not guilty?"

The prisoner responded with rapidity, "not guilty, sir."

The Court then said: "Call the jury, Mr. Sheriff."

At this juncture, the sister of the prisoner, Mrs. Nafey of New Brunswick, NJ., came into the courtroom and went up to the dock and the prisoner arising with bright smiles, grasped her sister's hand and kissed her heartily while tears ran down her face. These she suppressed quickly, and immediately afterward shook hands with her brother-in-law, who then came up and kissed him, and she did the same to a brother, Mr. Joseph Danbury of New Brunswick.

The jurymen were the following-named: Messrs. Horace Thompson, Almon P. Rowe, Dwight W. Tuttle, Eli Parmele, Ira A. Doolittle, Leonard Doolittle, Hiram Wooding, Edward N. Potter, Philo Bradley, Chauncey Williard, John Williard, Walter Hough.

THE TRIAL.

Dr. Beardsley of Derby was the first witness called. He gave his testimony as follows:

"I was the family physician of Sherman and was called to see the deceased Tuesday, May 9th, 1871 when the prisoner met me and expressed her anxiety to see me. Sherman told me that he thought he had one of his old turns; I found his symptoms to be nausea, vomiting, parched mouth and throat, great thirst, sharp pain in stomach, racking pain in bowels, hot, dry skin, quick pulse and some faintness; was told that he had been off on a spree of a week and came home sick. In reply to my question why Mrs. Sherman gave her husband money, she said that she had some trouble with him, that he had spent $1,200 or $1,500 of her money, and that she had tried to control him in vain. I gave him one-eighth gram morphine and a one gram blue pill to be taken every two hours; he said that upon the previous night he had been taken with severe pain in the head, followed by nausea and vomiting until I saw him; he said he had eaten a light supper and had eaten nothing unusual. I gave him a prescription and some directions in regard to treatment during the night and departed. I saw him at 11 P. M., and found him no better, with symptoms same as before. I took precautions in regard to night and left; on Wednesday morning there appeared a lull in the degree of severity in symptoms; vomiting, thirst, etc., etc., were less severe; this was Wednesday, A. M., March 10th. When I prescribed cooling drinks, means to obtain an evacuation and measures to relieve pain; that evening all of the symptoms were aggravated; the matter thrown from the stomach was dark and offensive; breath heavy; retained hardly anything on the stomach; mouth and throat very red; respiration quick; complained of faintness; constantly hawking and choking, loss of voice so that he could not speak above a whisper; I gave him brandy and water; Thursday, A.M. Sherman was decidedly worse, and symptoms pointed to fatal termination; pulse imperceptible; extremities cold; cold all over; complained of being faint; burning pain in the pit of his stomach; these symptoms were not from a debauch or ordinary disease; both Mr and Mrs. Sherman said that nothing had been administered, save what was ordered — that is, the sling and soothing drinks. Thursday morning, in reply to a question from the deceased, I told him that I feared he had his last sickness; he thought himself that he was going to die; I said I did not understand this intolerable thirst, vomiting, and other symptoms, and asked him if he had taken anything; he said nothing except that which was ordered, and that his wife had been particular to do as directed. Thursday evening, Dr. Kinney was called in consultation, and in my absence gave a recipe of composed mostly of subnitrate of bismuth[4]; this was administered to him that night, but I then expressed the opinion that nothing would save Mr. Sherman. All he took that night was Dr. Kinney's prescription, brandy and water, and little of that. Friday morning at sunrise, he saw him again; he was then apparently in a dying state; he died about eight o'clock A. M. There was a livid appearance of skin, especially under the eyes; all leading symptoms which correspond to those originating from poisoning by arsenic. Three symptoms which I have seen

4. Has been used to treat duodenal ulcers and is an anti-diarrheic agent

present in cases of arsenic poison were absent from this case, viz., purging, delirium and convulsions. Between nine and ten o'clock A.M. on Friday, Dr. Kinney came over to our village and called at the house where I was detained and called me out. We then had free interchange of opinion as to the cause of Sherman's death; my own opinion was that everything pointed to poisoning by arsenic; I determined on a post-mortem examination with a view to find out contents in the stomach. I sent a note by Dr. Kinney to the prisoner requesting, as her family physician, a post-mortem examination of her husband; she readily assented to examination. Dr. Kinney procured necessary legal papers, and the examination was made Saturday morning May 13th, about 10 A.M. Drs. Kinney, Shelton, and myself were the only persons present; body exposed externally; no unusual appearance presented; integument over stomach dissected; stomach and duodenum or lesser stomach removed; the stomach proper seemed empty except of gas; ligature placed about the upper orifice and also lower orifice and removed from body. We then examined by holding up to light and manipulation, and we found places of inflammation and ulceration; the stomachs then rolled up in white muslin cloth and tied; then put them in a large glass jar never used, the cloth and jar having been procured by Dr. Kinney for this purpose. The liver had a normal appearance. The right and left lobes and gall removed, about half of the liver; this portion of liver was rolled up in muslin[5] and put in a box, locked, and sent to New Haven for examination intestinal canals then examined. A section of transverse arch of colon was removed, opened, and internal coating showed marks of inflammation. I don't remember that this removed portion was put in a bottle; the brain was not examined, as all symptoms pointed to trouble in the stomach, not in the heart, lungs or brain. Mr. Sherman had "turns" on 9th of December, and other times after sprees, and this sickness and vomiting, were not unlike in Sherman's opinion "the old turns."

The question here arose between counsel as to the admission of Sherman's statements, that he thought the sickness by which he was dying was like previous cases. The court decided that prosecution

5. Lightweight cotton cloth

could prove the last attack was unlike previous cases, but Sherman's statements in reference to past cases was not admissible.

Symptoms of Sherman's last sickness, in the main, were unlike previous cases, except in nausea, vomiting, and thirst. These symptoms were like those of December 9th, 1870 and May 9th, insatiable thirst, burning throat, intense pain in the pit of the stomach, griping pain in bowels hurried respiration. These were unlike the symptoms of December 9th. In my opinion, he did not die of any natural disease, taking the symptoms from day to day from the time I saw him to his death, post-mortem examination, and chemical analysis. I have no doubt that Sherman's death was caused from poison — I think white arsenic or ratsbane. Mrs. Sherman had full charge of him, she said she could get along with him without other help. She was always in the room and apparently did what she could for him. In my opinion the recurrence of symptoms after abatement was caused by the administration of another dose of poison.

SEVENTH DAY.[6]

The proceedings on Thursday, April 25th, the seventh day of the trial of Lydia Sherman, proved of more interest to the public than any that have occurred. The courtroom opened with a full audience and remained crowded throughout the day. The delivery of the arguments of the four counsel occupied the entire day. There were able presentations of the case in different phases and were listened to with unflagging interest by both jury and spectators. The prisoner who was watched close by the throng of people present, paid very little attention to anything except the words of the counsel. She seemed more than at any time we have observed her, deeply impressed with the gravity of her situation. Before the court opened, she wept a little, and at nearly all the touching references made by the counsel in their remarks, particularly those by her own counsel, she shed tears. The proceedings were begun by
COL. WM.B. WOOSTERS ARGUMENT.

---

6. The trial was back and forth trying to come to a verdict

The argument in the main was very labored and dragged along wearily. But one good point made by the counsel was the fact of the prisoner buying arsenic so openly and inquiring how to use it. She could have come to New Haven and purchased it without any fear of detection. Indeed, the state would never had known that she had arsenic in her possession had she not frankly declared the fact and stated candidly the motive for which it was so secured — to poison rats. The last act of his life in giving into her care, in the presence of God and man, the custody of his favorite boy, shows that, no matter what others may have observed or felt to be their angry disagreements, Sherman passed from this life with a loving confidence in his wife. At a quarter past two, Judge Foster and the state prosecutor commenced to review the evidence. After disclaiming any intention to put in any evidence not authorized by the practice, the counsel considered the points made in Mr. Gardener's summing up. The accused, he said, was accused of murder, and as the attorney is compelled to charge in the indictment the particular degree, and all cases of poison under the law come under the designation of murder in the first degree. He had no alternative in this case but to charge the higher offence; still the jury had the power to bring in a verdict of murder in the second degree. To convict, the state must show first that Sherman died; second, that he died of poison; third, that it was administered by the accused, and fourth, that it was done with felonious intent. The first has been proved beyond a doubt. In support of the second it appears he entered the house a healthy man; the accused prepared and gave him food, and him alone — the other members of the family being away went out, and within an hour was taken with an attack that carried him off. She alone tended him in his illness, and we say she killed him! What can be added to carry conviction to the mind of her guilt, except we produce someone who swears they mixed the poison or saw it mixed by her? This man was well; took food and chocolate at the hands of his wife, sickened and died, and poison was found in his body. That is our case. Is it not plain and intelligible? The last point is intent. The rule is that the defence must show the motive. Mrs. Sherman has not done so, and it is fair to presume it was done with felonious intent. The case presents domestic relations of an unhappy character, distrust, coldness and jealousy, so much so that when Sherman's corpse lay there, the prisoner said to his mother, "I had resolved to leave Nelson, but now I am glad I did not." This shows that their domestic relations were not happy. The defence had declared that life had never been taken upon the testimony of a single expert, and the prisoner should not be convicted on the single testimony of Dr. Barker. Mr. Foster gave a French precedent in Elwell, where a person was hung on analysis of one exhibiting poison after two had failed to find any.

EIGHTH DAY.

Judge Park began the proceedings on Friday April 26th by charging the jury. He charged strongly against the prisoner but pointed out the fact to the jury that they could find her guilty of murder in the second degree. This they did after an absence of fifty minutes. The penalty is imprisonment for life. The prisoner pressed her hand to her forehead and sat down, her son at her side. She was calm again in a moment and conversed with her friends as though nothing unusual had happened. She was led out by Jailor Webster, followed by a crowd that blocked the street. She stepped into an open buggy and was drawn to the jail.

THE CONFESSION OF AN UNNATURAL
WIFE AND MOTHER.

Contrary to general opinion, Lydia Sherman was only convicted of murder in the second degree, but exception was taken to the evidence by her counsel, and sentence was not given at the time. Since the trial, Mrs. Sherman has been confined in the county jail, where she drew up a confession of the murders she committed by poisoning with arsenic. The scene in court was unaccompanied by any affecting incidents, and after the delivery of the charge, the prisoner was immediately placed in a sleigh and driven back to the county jail, whence she will soon be taken to Wethersfield, to be there imprisoned for the period of her natural life.

THE CONFESSION.

I was born near the town of Burlington, NJ., Dec. 24, 1824. My mother died when I was nine years old, and I was sent to live with my uncle, Mr. John Claygay. I never attended school much, being able to go only about three months in the year. At 16 years of age, I went to New Brunswick with my two brothers, and afterward to live with the Rev. Mr. Van Amburg in Jacksonville, twenty-five miles from New Brunswick. I lived there for three years, then returned to New Brunswick and learned to be a tailoress. I worked three months without pay and was then employed by a Mr. Owen. He was a class leader in the Methodist church of which I became a member. It was there that I met Mr. Edward Struck, who was a devoted Christian up to a few months before his death. I was his wife eighteen years; he has been dead about eight years. Our first child we called Lydia, and after her birth we went to New York and resided near Elizabeth and Houston Street. In New York we had two boys. Afterward we moved to Carmansville, where we had four children born. At the end of that time, Mr. Struck obtained an appointment on the Metropolitan Police force. Six months later we lost a daughter, aged twenty-two months, by the measles. About this time, my husband was transferred to Manhattanville, and we moved to 125th street. Then occurred our first trouble, which came about in this way:

A man came up to Stratton's Hotel, on the Bloomingdale Road, and made a disturbance in the bar-room. He attacked the bartender with a knife and immediately the cry of murder was sounded. Just at this time, the Manhattanville stage came along and on it was a detective who heard the cry. He rushed into the hotel but finding he was powerless to accomplish anything, he asked for the assistance of a policeman. There was none near, and he endeavored to quiet the man by talking to him, but he could not succeed. The man appeared deranged. The detective struck him with a cane, but the man would not desist. He struck the officer with a knife, when the latter drew a pistol and shot the man.

The stage drove on and soon met Mr. Struck, and as he was a policeman, the driver told him the circumstances about the killing of the man at the hotel. Mr. Struck started immediately for the hotel, and when he reached there, he found that the man was dead. Word was sent to the Manhattanville police station and the doctors gave it as their opinion that the man was deranged. My husband reported at headquarters, and soon after a rumor prevailed that he would not arrest the man because he had a pistol. This was incorrect, but the employees of the hotel testified that Mr. Struck was at the place and was afraid to go in. The result was that he was discharged from the police force. I sent for Capt. Hart, but when he came my husband would neither look, speak, nor have anything to do with him. The captain said he was out of his mind and advised me to have him sent to an asylum.

One night after this, he was acting very badly and I called in the police sergeant who lived in the lower part of our house. The sergeant advised me to put him out of the way, as he would never be any good to me or himself again. I asked him what he meant, and he told me to get a certain quantity of arsenic and give him some of it. I paid ten cents for it, put it in some oaf meal gruel, and gave him some of it during the afternoon. That night he was very ill, and at 8 o'clock the next morning he died.

The following July I made up my mind that my two little children, Mary Ann, six years old, and Edward, two years younger, would be better off if they were out of the way, so after thinking the matter over for several days, I made them some of the same kind of gruel their father had eaten. They only survived a short time.

The doctors said that the children died of gastric fever. They had not the least suspicion of the truth.

I continued to keep the house and had four children with me at the time. My son, George Whitfield, who was then 14 years of age, was living with me. In the latter part of August, he was taken sick, and I sent for Dr. Oviatt. He said the boy had painters colic, and as he did not improve, I became discouraged, and mixed some arsenic in his tea. He died the next day, and the doctor said it was painters colic.

Then my little daughter Ann Eliza took the chills and fever and was continually sick. This made me downhearted and discouraged again. I had some arsenic in the house which I purchased in Harlem, and I put it in the medicine I bought for her to cure the chills. I gave it to her twice, then she was taken sick as the others were, and died about noon four days afterward. She was the happiest child I ever saw.

I then kept the house until the following May going out as usual to do nursing. About that time, Lydia, my eldest daughter, went to New York with work, was taken sick, and after an illness of 21 days she died a natural death. I never gave her anything the doctor did not order. Then I went to Sailorsville, PA., with a family named Maxom. It was not a profitable venture, so I returned to New York and went to live with my step-daughter, Mrs. Thompson. Then I took a situation with Mr. Cochran, who kept a sewing machine establishment on Canal Street. There I became acquainted with Mr. James Curtis. He asked me to go to Stratford, CT., to take care of his aged mother and keep house for them. I consented to go for $8.00 per month. I lived there eight months. One day Mr. John Fairchild, at whose store I bought our groceries, asked me if I would like to keep house for a man who had just lost his wife. In this way I became acquainted with Mr. Hurlburt, who lived in Coram, Huntington. After I had been a few days with him he asked me to marry him, which I did November 22, 1868. The ceremony was performed by the Rev. Mr. Morton in his own house. We lived happily for fourteen months. About three months after we were married, Mr. Hurlburt made his will; he was subject to fits of dizziness.

One day he was unwell, and he ate clams and drank cider with saleratus[7] in it. Then he became worse. On one occasion he made me drink cider and saleratus, after which I became very sick and dizzy, and I took to vomiting. Finally, Mr. Hurlburt became worse, and about 5 o'clock one morning the old man died. Now I wish to say that I never gave Mr. Hurlburt anything that would cause sickness, though there may have been arsenic mixed with the saleratus which he put into the cider.

About two months after Hurlburt died, I heard that Horatio N. Sherman of Birmingham wanted me to take a little baby to board. I met Mr. Sherman one Sunday morning. He introduced himself to me and said that he had another object in calling besides getting me to take care of his baby. He wanted me as his housekeeper, because his mother-in-law and his daughter could not get along well together, I said I would think about it. Two weeks later he came again and offered to marry me. I told him we ought to be better acquainted. He said that he was compelled to get someone, as he could not have the old woman in the house, as she was creating a constant disturbance. He then went away, and I did not see him for three or four weeks; but at the end of that time he found me a tenant for my farm, which ended in my lending him $300.

In July 1870, I lent him $300 more, and on the 3rd of September 1870, we went to Mr. Sherman's sister's house, in Bridgewater. MA. and were married. After we had been married about two months, Mr. Sherman said he wished his babe Frank would die, as then the old woman should not stay another day in the house. I was full of trouble, and not knowing what to do, I was tempted to give Franky something to get him out of the way, for I thought he would be better off. They had arsenic in the house; the old lady had used it before to poison rats. I put some of it in some milk and only gave it to him once. Being quite feeble, he began to be sick and to vomit. I sent for a doctor, but he said the child was not out of danger, though he was better. This was in the forenoon. That night the child died at 11 o'clock, his was November 15, 1870.

7. Sodium bicarbonate; main ingredient of baking powder

Mr. Sherman then took to drink, and I supported the family for about six months. During this time, I found that he had dissipated the money I gave him instead of paying his bills with it, so I had to pay out about $300 more for him. Then came Christmas, and Ada devoted a great deal of time in decorating the church. I furnished her with all her clothes and paid her dressmaking bills. On Christmas Eve, Ada was taken sick and Dr. Beardsley was again sent for. He prescribed a brand sling for her, but Mr. Sherman drank all the liquor I bought. I could not keep a drop for Ada. The next morning, she was no better, and we sent for Dr. Dutton of Milford. When the doctor came, Mr. Sherman was so drunk that he could not walk straight. Mr. Sherman asked me for $10 to pay the doctor. I refused to give it to him, saying that I would pay the doctor myself. Then he got mad and went out.

That made me feel so bad that I was tempted to do as I had done before. I had some arsenic in the house which I mixed in her tea and gave her twice. She died the next morning.

Then Mr. Sherman began drinking more than ever. Sunday, he went out and returned very drunk. Monday, he went out again and returned in the evening. He drank a cup of chocolate and then went out to get some greens for dinner.

While he was gone, he was taken sick and he came home immediately. I had about a pint of brandy in the house, and I put some arsenic in it. That night he drank it and the next morning he was very sick. I did not mean to kill him, I only wanted to make him sick of liquor. The next day he drank more of the brandy and was worse. I sent for Dr. Beardsley and told him that Mr. Sherman had one of his old spells. He continued to grow worse, other doctors were called in, but he died at 8 o'clock the following morning.

THE FAMILY FEUD. RAGE OF MR. SHERMAN'S MOTHER
AND THE TERRIBLE ACUSATIONS — " HE WAS POSIONED."

Jesse Harding Pomeroy

(November 29, 1859- September 29, 1932)

HE WAS AN AMERICAN SERIAL KILLER and the youngest person in the history of the Commonwealth of Massachsetts to be convicted of murder in the first degree. He was found guilty of murder by a jury trial held in the Supreme Judicial Court of Suffolk County in December 1874. He had murdered and mutilated 4-year-old Horace II. Milieu and 10-year-old Katie Curran.

Pomeroy was born in Boston, Massachusetts to Thomas J. Pomeroy and Ruth Ann Snowman. He also had an older brother named Charles Jefferson Pomeroy.

Jesse had been fascinated with tormenting and torturing young boys. He cut them with knives. He used the excuse that he could not help himself and that an "unknown power seized him, and he was changed." Pomeroy was sentenced to solitary life imprisonment on September 9, 1870, at 17-years-old.

While in prison, he would read and paint. He went on to study languages: French, German, and Latin. He kept to himself but got in trouble with the officers most because of his attempts to escape. However, on November 9, 1877, he tried to escape by digging through the mortar in his cell. After this, he made about 12 attempted escapes; numerous handmade tools were discovered in his cell. Eventually, he broke out of his cell but was recaptured. On average, he received six and a half day punishments each year for tampering with his cell to escape. Another time he got himself in trouble because he refused to obey an order, and another for writing a disrespectful letter to the warden.

In 1920, Pomeroy published poems in the prison newspaper. Later, he published a book of poetry and prose after arguing with the officers for his right to have them published. His book called, Selections from the Writing of Jesse Harding Pomeroy, Life Prisoner Since 1874 in which he writes about prison, literature, his hopes, thoughts, and his experiences.

By 1929, Pomeroy, an elderly man, had been transferred to Bridgewater Hospital for the Criminally Insane where he died on September 29, 1932 at age 72.

TIMELINE

1859 -On November 29th, Jesse Harding Pomeroy is born

1871 -Jesse traps and attacks seven young boys
-In April, he is put on trial and arrested for the attacks
-Jesse is sent to Westborough reform school

1874 -In March, Jesse kidnaps and kills 10-year-old Katie Curran
-In April, Jesse murders 4-year-old Horace Mullen Jesse
-He is put on trial and found guilty in December

1875 -Jesse recieves a death penalty sentence in February

1876 -In August, there is a revote to his sentence and Jesse is
sentenced to life in prison
-On September 7th, Jesse is sent to state prison at Charlestown

1814 -Jesse makes roughly 12 escape attempts while in prison

1929 -He is transferred to Bridgewater Hospital for the
Criminally Insane

1932 -On September 29, he dies at age 72 at the hospital

The Life
Of
Jesse Harding Pomeroy

THE MOST REMARKABLE CASE IN THE HISTORY OF CRIME OR CRIMINAL LAW.

BY E. LUSCOMB HASKELL. ILLUSTRATED.
BOSTON: 1892.

THE CONTEXTS.

ILLUSTRATIONS.

CHAPTER I.

POMEROY'S CLOSE CONFINEMENT IN THE
MASSACHUSETTS STATE PENAL INSTITUTIONS.

THERE CAN BE NO DOUBT that the most interesting convict in
the Commonwealth of Massachusetts, if not in the whole country,
is Jesse Harding Pomeroy.

He is the only convict in the United States who is absolutely
consigned to a cage, and who is looked upon by the community as
a veritable fiend.

For years he has been an inmate of the Massachusetts State
Prison and has been a constant source of trouble and annoyance to
the officers of the institution.

His history is interesting, for he is a person with very
marked characteristics. There are peculiar people, those with
hobbies and who are often called "cranks," who are met with
every day. — Some of them have a leaning toward one thing
and some another. It has been said that such persons were born
with these peculiarities and that they have no control over their
actions when directed in the line of their characteristics. It is a
question with not a few intelligent men and women whether a

person should be punished for doing a thing which he or she could not help.

It must be admitted that when the inclinations of an individual are such that the community is endangered, it is a public duty for the proper officers to take charge of such a person.

Whatever then may be the opinion of anyone in regard to the punishment inflicted on the subject of this book, certain it is that the public is better satisfied and feels a greater security with Pomeroy safe behind the bars of the prison.

There are those who do not believe in solitary confinement of convicts. This statement is corroborated by a letter published by a prominent New York daily newspaper, of which the following is an abstract:

"Solitary confinement of refractory criminals in prisons or reformatories, or of the inmates of lunatic asylums, is unquestionably just and wise,. But solitary confinement for a long term of years of a human being in a normal state of mind would seem to be more in the nature of a torture worthy only of the middle ages.

Solitary confinement, or what is in reality isolation in Pomeroy's case, to the average mind is most terrible. And yet what could be done with Pomeroy if he was allowed the privileges of the prison, the same as other convicts?

Neither the prison officials nor the public would tolerate his being given an opportunity to be at large even behind the high walls of the institution. It might be possible that he would make a successful escape.

Such is the feeling in regard to this one man that mothers especially would be in a constant state of alarm from fear that he would escape and do irreparable injury to children, or that he would at the first opportunity commit another murder.

It is, therefore, desirable that this convict should continue in a condition of isolation inside the granite walls of the Massachusetts State Prison. It is far better that one individual should suffer than that the community should be placed in fear. Even the fact that he is in close confinement is not wholly satisfactory to many reputable citizens. They are not backward in expressing their belief that the Commonwealth would have been far better off had he been executed soon after the time of his conviction, rather than that the death sentence should have been commuted to close confinement for life in the state prison.

There is a limit to human endurance. It is not well to bestow too much charity on such a man as Pomeroy.

Time, as is well known, tends to soften the asperities of the human heart and often leads one to condone grievous faults. It is well, under all circumstances, to examine into the causes which lead to the condition of affairs, weigh the evidence on both sides, and award a verdict in accordance with the facts. The one-sided view taken by not a few in regard to criminals does not benefit the community which must be protected from the evil disposed. Law must be respected.

The general condemnation of Pomeroy has, doubtless, prevented the circulation of a petition for his pardon, or to allow him some of the privileges enjoyed by the other convicts. His crimes were outrageous. Had it not been for his youth, he would have paid the penalty for his offences on the scaffold.

He took a fiendish delight in tormenting and torturing boys, who were younger than himself. When asked why he did so, he would reply that he 'could not help it.' Some unknown power seized him and he was changed, almost instantly, from a boy in his teens to a devil, he loved to witness the effects of his cruel acts and would dance in glee around the victim he had selected for his horrible pleasure. These facts would have seemed impossible of belief had it not been for the testimony, which was introduced at the trial, and the admittance of its truth by the counsel for the defence.

The point which the counsel sought to make was that while Pomeroy was guilty of atrocious murder, he was not responsible for his acts. That he was insane and that the jury should find him not guilty by reason of insanity. If the jury had returned such a verdict, it would have been obligatory upon the supreme judicial court to have sentenced the prisoner to one of the State asylums for the insane during his natural life. Very important evidence was presented on both sides, the most expert doctors on insanity being placed on the witness stand by the defence as well as by the government.

The jury, notwithstanding the able efforts of the counsel for the defence, returned a verdict of murder in the first degree. The evidence of the insanity experts was so contradictory that the jury could not well consider that the prisoner was insane although he was wanting in will power. In a few words, Pomeroy, when opportunity offered, would commit assaults, knowing at the time that he was doing wrong, and yet was not possessed of sufficient moral strength to resist the temptation. This has been the case with many criminals, but they have not been led to commit murder or to inflict torture. I bring to mind one man, now serving out a sentence in the Charlestown prison, this being his second term in that institution.

This man would be law-abiding so long as he abstained from the use of liquor. As soon as he became intoxicated, he would steal. It made no difference to him what article he purloined. He seemed to be impelled to commit a theft. When he had become sober and informed of what he had done, he could give no reason why he had stolen. There are convicts in the Massachusetts State Prison, and I doubt not, in similar institutions in other states, who steal every time a chance is offered. — They steal from each other. They love to steal; they cannot resist the desire. Whether this desire was born in them or acquired, I am unable to say.

It is not my intention in this history to enter into a lengthy discussion on the subject of Pomeroy's sanity. For is it my desire to comment on existing laws as regards the conviction and imprisonment of men and women, and children, who commit offences because they could not help it. The legislatures of the various states are ever endeavoring to make the laws more humane. — Whether these deliberative bodies have succeeded in this direction, it is for the public to judge. The community must not, however, be subjected to the evil acts of individuals, and of tailors against society must be punished whether or not they were impelled to commit the acts.

I do not want to be understood as being devoid of sympathy for the convict, confined in a penal institution under a heavy sentence. I have a very warm place in my heart for this class.

Some of the convicts in the Massachusetts bastille have occupied high places of trust, but in an unguarded moment turned from the path of honesty and then, in a shorter or longer period of time, reached the state prison.

In dealing with convicts, it must be kept in mind that they are human beings and should receive the sympathy and care of the State.

It is in this light that the case of Pomeroy should be viewed. He is a ward of the State and must be cared for as humanely as possible. It is well, however, that he is confined more closely than any of the other prisoners in the institution. The interests of the community are better subserved in this way. He is not likely to harm anyone in his present apartments and his incarceration has not, apparently, done him much injury. Jesse must be looked upon as being situated in the best possible manner for the public and himself.

I cannot do better, in order to give the reader valuable information, then to quote from an interesting pamphlet, entitled, "Criminals," written by Dr. Charles D. Sawin, former physician at the Massachusetts State Prison, and who had Pomeroy under his care for five years. The learned physician said:

"For the sake of refreshing the mind of the reader we will state that Pomeroy was tried and convicted in 1874 for the murder of a little boy four years and three months old, and during this trial it was proven that he had at various times been guilty of acts of the most atrocious cruelty towards other children. As the District Attorney stated in his opening address, this child when found possessed a body still warm, throat cut, and some fifteen or twenty stabs in the region of the heart.

The little boy's hands were wounded more or less; there were marks of wounds upon his arms, suggesting, perhaps, the possibility of feeble struggles to resist.

The government charged deliberate murder with malice aforethought and carried out with a considerable degree of atrocity and cruelty. A number of experts were called in and examined Jesse on various occasions previous to the trial. When actors disagree in their estimate of such a well-defined character as Hamlet, how it to be is wondered at that mental experts oiler such divergent views concerning the responsibility for his acts of such a young boy as Pomeroy, when playing on the stage of life.

Pomeroy entered the prison, his sentence having been commuted to solitary imprisonment for life, Sept. 9, 1870, when he was seventeen years old. During a portion of his term he has been permitted many privileges and diversions, such as reading and painting. At one time he evinced a strong desire to improve his mind, and he studied French, German and Latin. His knowledge of the languages is, however, only a smattering one. Of late, he has taken a special liking to chemistry, and a slight spark of inventive genius has been manifested in his endeavors to construct a hollow self-sharpening lead pencil, in which he takes great pride. His paintings are hardly worth admiring, but he looks upon them as works of art, this fact demonstrating to the observer that his standard is not very high. Without doubt, his intellect and moral sense must have improved to a certain degree, since he has not associated with other prisoners, and he hasn't passed through any stage of 'devolution.'

His first punishment in prison was four and a half days in a dark cell, on Nov. 9, 1877, for trying to escape, digging cement out of a cell.

On the average, he has received six and one-half days punishment each year, in most cases for tampering with his cell structure in attempting to escape. He, on one occasion, was punished for insolence to an officer; once for refusing to obey an order, and once 'for writing an insolent letter to the warden.' Not very serious offences these.

He has never exhibited his former love to torture at any time during his incarceration in prison, which seems rather strange were he insane at the time of the murders.

He is remarkably cunning, clever, and quick to see the drift of a conversation, logical and clear in understanding, but notably self-willed and persistent. His bodily health has been remarkably good, eating and sleeping well; seldom complaining of his diet and never asking for favors or extra rations.

In a recent interview, he stated that he thought his memory was very good in regard to some occurrences; as, for instance, his life in jail and his first four years in prison, but he had no recollection of ever meeting Dr. Folsom, and only an indistinct remembrance of his trial.

According to Dr. Sawin, Pomeroy has not suffered in bodily health during his many years of close confinement. Imprisonment for a long term of years has not, in numerous instances, proven harmful physically.

Jesse Pomeroy has never made any attempt to injure himself, he is very considerate concerning his person. If he ever did entertain a desire to commit suicide, which I think he never did, he must have been kept from attempting self-destruction the regal'd he has held for his relatives. Some of them have been very faithful to him. Their words have always been those of great encouragement.

I remember, quite a number of years ago, of reading a letter sent to Jesse. In it he was told to be good and true. He was requested to study and acquire knowledge. He was assured that he would not always be a prisoner, confined as he was, but that he would be released in time and would associate with people of the world at large. He was told that someday he might occupy a high position in society. The letter showed that there was someone who loved him, notwithstanding the bitterness of the world toward him. Although his hands had been bathed in human blood, there was an affection which had not been obliterated.

He has been visited by relatives whenever the regulations of the prison would admit. There can be no doubt that some of his relations have the kindest and most sympathetic feelings for him. The idea that he -was insane when he committed his cruel, atrocious and murderous acts is, doubtless, entertained by them.

CHAPTER II.

AN ACCOUNT OF THE DISCOVERY OF THE BODY
OF THE MURDERED MILLEN BOY.

TO FURNISH ACCURATE INFORMATION relative to the discovery of the body of the murdered Millen boy, for the commission of which crime Pomeroy was arrested, tried and convicted; and to show the intense feeling of the public, I have taken an account of it from the Boston Globe of Thursday, April 23, 1874. The reporter, it appears, was very careful in the presentation of the important facts. The recital of the story of the crime of nearly twenty years ago thrills the blood and arouses feelings of indignation. The reporter's story follows:

"A murder, which, considered in view of all its horrible attending circumstances, perhaps, surpasses in cold-blooded atrocity any deed of its nature ever recorded, came to light, yesterday afternoon, at 5 o'clock, by the discovery of the body of the victim on the beach of Dorchester Bay, midway between South Boston and Savin Hill. The murdered person was a boy, four and a half years old, named Horace H. Millen, whose father resides at 253 Dorchester Street. The first intimation which the authorities had of the affair was when a deaf-mute boy, of about fourteen years, came up to Officer Lyons of Station 9 drawing his hand across his throat and mysteriously pointing in the direction of the place mentioned.

The officer hardly knew what to make of the boy's motions, but finally concluded to follow him, and presently came upon the explanation, the corpse of a then unknown child, lying within a circle of stones piled up for a clambake. The throat was cut from ear to ear, an ugly stab had completely put out the left eye, a deep wound had completely severed the jugular vein, and subsequent investigation exposed the horrible fact that eighteen stabs, forming a circle of about three inches diameter, about the breast, had been made with some instrument like an awl, or a remarkably slender knife blade, and that with a view to severing an artery a stab had been indicted, penetrating the groin to a considerable depth.

The deaf-mute had been playing about the swamp and beach and having discovered the body, had hastened to inform the first officer whom he should meet.

The body was at once taken to Station 9, and by the direction of Coroner Allen was delivered to Undertaker Waterman. The news was received at the Chief's office at a little after 5 o'clock and measures were at once set on foot for the unravelling of the mystery. The first fact ascertained was that the boy's name was Millen. Information had been given at Station 0. In South Boston, that Horace H. Millen was missing. The description given of him coincided exactly with the appearance of the murdered child. The size, age, colors of hair and eyes and dress were exactly alike, and, when the coroner waited upon the bereaved parents and gave a minute description than had previously been given, the fact was clear. The boy had not been seen since 10 o'clock in the forenoon, at which time he was at play with his mates at the corner of Dorchester and Eighth streets. — He did not come home to dinner and as the hours went by, without his making an appearance, his parents became more and more alarmed and were preparing to fear the worst when the awful tidings reached them.

This much ascertained, of course, the next question had to do with the murderer. Here there was nothing to guide the inquirer except mere guess work. It seemed to be the impression among

the detectives that no person of sane mind could have committed the murder, so inhumanely cruel, so unnecessary to the execution of any intent were those horrid mutilations. A lunatic, possibly, might take delight in such barbarity, but another explanation seemed more probable. Someone recollected a horrible tragedy enacted about two years ago in Chelsea, which those, who had read at the time, must certainly re-call now. Indeed, one could hardly soon forget a crime so outrageous.

An East Boston boy was enticed from his home and taken to the seclusion of Powder Horn Hill, where he was found tied fast to a tree and cut, and stabbed, so terribly that, after the most excruciating suffering, he died within a very short time. The fiend who perpetrated this diabolical deed, was a boy named Pomeroy, who was tried, convicted and sentenced to two years at Westboro. The similarity of the two murders was so great that it seemed almost a logical conclusion that they were the work of 'one and the same hand.' These were the impressions which prevailed soon after the discovery of the murder.

Late at night, of the day of the commission of the crime. Sergeant Lucas and Patrolman Adams of Station 6, South Boston. Arrested Pomeroy and locked him up to answer to a charge of willful and deliberate murder.

The next day Detective Woods took Jesse to the warerooms of the undertaker where had been placed the remains of the Millen boy. Jesse was put in a position so that he could look upon the body of his victim. He turned his head from the sight became pale and trembled.

Several questions were asked the prisoner, in substance, as follows:

"Was you acquainted with this little boy?"

"Yes sir, I was," replied Jesse.

"Did you cause his death?"

"I suppose I did, sir."

"How did you get the blood from the knife; did you wash it off?"

"No, sir. I kept sticking it in the mud until it was clean and there was no blood on it."

At the conclusion of the interview Pomeroy was taken to the

Suffolk County jail on Charles Street, Boston, to await the action of the coroner's jury.

The preliminary inquest, commonly known as the view, was held at Undertaker Waterman's, under the supervision of Coroner Allen. The jury was composed of the following named gentlemen: William P. Wentworth, foreman, Benjamin Bracket, Byron Lord.S. D. Waugh. J. F. Pond and G. W. Downs. — The investigation revealed only what has been previously stated; but it seemed to be the impression of the jury that the wounds 35. About the heart were inflicted in the way of torture. The little boy's hands were badly cut, from which it was inferred that he had put them up to ward off the strokes of the knife, or other instrument, and that his tormentor had rebuked him by an occasional slashing cut. Death, it was thought, was produced by a stab in the neck which severed the jugular vein, and that the fatal wound was, probably, not given until the murderer's cruel propensities had been completely cloyed.

The public was deeply interested in every detail of the horrible affair and anxious awaited the result of the inquest. On Tuesday evening, April 29, 1874, the following verdict was rendered by the coroner's jury:

"Horace Holden Millen came to his death between 11 o'clock in the forenoon and 5 o'clock in the afternoon of Wednesday, the 22d of April 1874, from loss of blood and injuries received in the neck and chest, which injuries were produced by some sharp, or cutting, instrument.

And the jury further find, upon the testimony before them, that they have probable cause to believe that said murder was committed by one Jesse Harding Pomeroy.

The verdict was very warmly endorsed by the public.

It should be stated that at the inquest Pomeroy accounted for his whereabouts on the day of the murder. He said he had never seen the Millen boy until he was brought before the body. He also denied that he had made a confession.

Meanwhile the funeral of the murdered boy had taken place. Rev. Mr. Rand officiated. The remains were taken to Wiscasset. Maine and buried. The fellow-workmen of Mr. Millen gave him a purse of $50 and the officers attached to Station G, South Boston, presented the grief-stricken parents with $150 in money.

An attendant at the inquest thus described Pomeroy:

"He sat quite unmoved in his chair, telling his story without embarrassment. He is a hoy a little more than live feet high, slim, straight, and when standing with his face averted presents a very good appearance. It is his face that tells the story of his life. To one who has studied the human countenance, a glance is sufficient. He sees in a moment how it was possible for him to perpetrate the outrages for which he was first taken into custody, and can readily believe him guilty of the horrible murder of which he is now charged. The cast of the right eye has nothing to do with this impression. They are wicked eyes sullenly, brutish wicked eyes, and as in moments of wandering thought the boy looks out of them he seems one, who could delight in

The writhings of his helpless victims beneath the stab of the knife, the puncture of the awl, or the prick of the pin, as he so often has delighted.

There is nothing interesting in the look. It is altogether unsympathetic, merciless. But more than all the rest is the sensuality that hangs like lead about those sunken eyes, and that marks every feature and contour of the face. The pallor of his complexion, the lifeless, flabby look that pertains to his cheeks, correspond with this view; and when the boy walks it is not the bold, buoyant movement of an innocent lad. But apparently the shuffling of one whose thoughts are of the lowest kind.

On Saturday, April 27, 1874, Pomeroy was brought before the Highland District Court, Boston, and charged with the murder of the Millen boy. He pleaded not guilty and was committed to jail without bail till the next Friday, May 1, to await the result of the inquest. When he next appeared in the lower court, he waived examination and was again committed to jail; this time to await the Grand Jury. This body returned a bill of willful murder against him. His next hearing was before the Supreme Judicial Court of Massachusetts.

CHAPTER III.
FINDING OF THE HIDDEN REMAINS OF KATIE CURRAN IN A CELLAR IN SOUTH BOSTON.

WHILE THE EXCITEMENT WAS at its height in regard to the brutal murder of the Millen boy there were many inquiries in relation to the whereabouts of a little girl, named Katie Curran, who had been missing for some length of time. Search was made almost everywhere for the child, but without success.

The state of the public mind can, therefore, be better imagined than described, when the announcement was made that the decomposed remains of a child had been discovered in the cellar of the store occupied by the Pomeroys in South Boston.

Immense crowds quickly congregated in the vicinity of the store. Had not the people had that respect for law and order characteristic of New England, Judge Lynch would, undoubtedly, have held high carnival at the time.

As it was, the police, fearing an uprising of the populace, took into custody the mother and her son, Charles, in order that the temptation for lynching one or both might be removed. — Crowds gathered about Station 6, South Boston, and it was some time before quietness was restored.

By the kindness of the genial and popular editor of the South Boston Inquirer, Mr. Charles L. Storrs, I was granted the privilege of consulting the files of his interesting weekly newspaper. From that publication I quoted the following account of the finding of the body of the little Curran girl, the date being July 20, 1874:

"Last Saturday afternoon the community was startled and shocked by the information that the body of Katie Curran, who has been missing since March 18, had been found in a cellar in Broadway.

The scene of the terrible tragedy and the horrible revelation was the premises 327 Broadway. The remains were discovered in a corner of the cellar, in a sort of recess made by a water closet and the foundation wall.

The body was partially covered with ashes and stones and was found by a workman who was employed in removing the wall. The remains were in such a state of decay as to prevent identification.

Word having been sent to the police station. Officer Adams, who came up with Officer Foote, recognized some of the clothing as belonging to Katie Curran.

Coroner Ingalls and Undertaker Cole were called in and the parents of the child were sent for.

Mrs. Curran at once recognized the clothing as being that of her Katie when she was missed.

Chief of Police Savage was sent for and on his arrival he immediately ordered the arrest of Mrs. Pomeroy and her son, Charles. Officer Adams took Mrs. Pomeroy to the station and Charles was arrested later by Officers Mountain and Deveney, upon his return from carrying his evening papers. Both were taken to the station, partly as important witnesses and partly to protect them from violence by enraged and threatening people.

By direction of Coroner Ingalls, Constable Lockwood summoned as a jury Messrs. I. T. Campbell, James Malcom, Thomas Gogin, Bernard Jenney, Charles H. Hersey and E. IH. Gill.

Sunday forenoon the Coroner and jury visited the premises and viewed the remains, which had been taken to the City Point tomb. The next day, Monday, in the afternoon, witnesses were heard.

The witnesses heard at the inquest were:

Mrs. Kate Curran.
Mr. John Curran.
Chief of Police Savage.
Mrs. Ruth Ann Pomeroy, then 33 years old.
Master Charles J. Pomeroy, brother of Jesse.
Sergeant Hood of Station 9.
Miss Emma Lee, 6 years old.
Special Officer Edward Mitchell, on duty on Chester Square.
Sergeant Emerson, and Officers Thomas H. Adams, Asel B. Griggs and Dennis Mountain, all of Station 6.
Miss Minnie Chapman, a girl who lived with Mrs. Pomeroy. Messrs. Charles McGinnis, John B. Margeson, John Foote, Thomas Gogin, James Nash, Thomas Tobin and William B. Rohr; and Mrs. W. E. Margeson and Miss Margaret Lane.

Most of the evidence was to the effect that the Curran girl was missed on a certain day and had not been seen alive since that time. The clothing, found on the body of the deceased, was identified as that worn by the child on the day she was missed.

There was very important evidence given by Chief of Police Savage, which was of such a positive character the murder of the Curran girl was traced directly to Jesse, and he, in addition to circumstantial evidence, admitted committing the deed and described how it was done.

The following excerpts from the testimony given at the inquest are interesting:

Chief Savage testified that after the arrest of Pomeroy some trivial circumstances came to his knowledge, which led him to instruct the captains of all the stations to search every cellar, well and by-way in their districts where there was even the remotest possibility that the body of the girl might be concealed.

He said that he gave special instructions to Captain Dyer to search the cellar of the Pomeroy's; and upon Captain Dyer informing him that his orders had been obeyed the Chief said he became satisfied.

The Chief stated that he was in South Boston after the body was discovered. He found the feeling so strong against

Mrs. Pomeroy that he deemed it advisable to order her to be taken into custody.

He also said that he had interviewed Pomeroy at Charles Street jail after the finding of the remains of the Curran girl. — At the interview the following dialogue ensued:

Chief. — "Jesse, do you know me?"

Pomeroy. — "Yes. Sir."

Chief. — "What do you suppose I came to see you about?"

Pomeroy. — "To talk about that case."

Chief. — "What case?"

Pomeroy. — "The case of the little boy."

Chief. — "No; I came to tell you that Katie Curran has been found buried in your mother's cellar. Your mother and brother have been arrested for the murder. Can you tell anything about it?"

Pomeroy hesitated, choked and replied, "No."

The chief said he made another visit when Jesse said: "Mr. Savage, I killed her but don't want to tell how."

After some additional conversation with the prisoner Chief Savage was agreeably surprised to find that Jesse would make a full confession of his horrible murder of the innocent little Curran girl.

Pomeroy at once proceeded to make a rough plan of the cellar where the body was found. He then began the narration of a story which illustrated his extreme disregard for human life. His confession was in substance as follows:

"I opened mother's store the day of the murder at about 7:30 o'clock. The girl came in for a paper. I told her there was a store down stairs. She went down to about the middle of the cellar and stood facing Broadway. I followed her. I put my arm around her neck, my hand over her mouth, and with my knife cut her throat, holding the knife in my right hand. I then dragged her behind the water closet, laying her head furthest up the place, and I put some stones and ashes oil the body. I took the ashes from a box in the cellar. I sent a boy into Hoyt & Lawrence's store, nearby and bought a knife for 25 cents. The knife was taken from me when I was arrested in April last. When I was in the cellar, I heard my brother at the outside door which I had locked after the girl came in. I ran up the stairs and saw him going towards the cellar in Mitchell's part.

He came back when he saw me. Two girls worked in the store for my mother. They usually got there about 9 o'clock in the morning. Mother got there later. Brother Charles and I took turns in opening the store till about April. My brother and mother never knew of this affair. I forgot to tell you that I washed my hands and knife, they being bloody, at the water pipe."

The evidence presented by Chief Savage was of itself sufficient to warrant the jury in returning a verdict charging the murder to Pomeroy. Other testimony was taken so that the investigation might be full and complete.

The inquest lasted several days. When all the testimony had been taken the jury, after considering the evidence, rendered a verdict as follows:

"That Katie M. Curran came to her death on or about the 18th of March 1874, at 327 Broadway, South Boston, by the hands of Jesse H. Pomeroy. He has acknowledged the crime, and all the evidence corroborates the statement.

The jury also found that either before or after the commission of the murder the girl's person was mutilated with a knife or some sharp instrument."

It was the circumstances attending the finding of the remains of the Curran girl which led to the resignation of Captain Dyer of Station 6. It will be noted that in his testimony at the Coroner's inquest Chief Savage stated that he gave special instructions to that officer in regard to searching for the missing girl. The cellar was said to have been searched, and Chief Savage was given to understand that fact and also that the missing girl had not been found. When the body was discovered the Captain left the station in charge of a lieutenant, because, it was stated, he had not the heart to look upon the scene of the murder.

Captain Dyer was summoned before Mayor Cobb of Boston and with few preliminaries the officer handed in his resignation.

$500
REWARD !

Mayor's Office, City Hall, April 1st, 1874.

In accordance with an order of the City Council, a reward of Five Hundred Dollars is hereby offered for the detection and conviction of the person or persons who on the 18th ultimo abducted from Broadway, South Boston,

KATIE MARY CURRAN,

aged about 10 years, the daughter of John and Mary Curran, residing in South Boston.

SAMUEL C. COBB, Mayor.

ROCKWELL & CHURCHILL, CITY PRINTERS, 122 WASHINGTON STREET, BOSTON.

CHAPTER IV.
THE TRIAL OF POMEROY FOR THE WILLFUL MURDER OF THE LITTLE MILLEN BOY.

ON TUESDAY, DEC. 12, 1874, Pomeroy was placed at the bar of the Supreme Judicial Court of Massachusetts to be tried for his life.

The clerk of the court read the indictment, charging him with the murder of the Millen boy.

Pomeroy pleaded not guilty.

Joseph H. Cotton, Esq., at present Associate Justice of the Municipal Court for the Charlestown District, had been the counsel for the defence.

When the case came to trial it was conducted by Hon. Charles Robinson, Jr., whose efforts in behalf of his client were characteristic of the able lawyer. He devoted his best energies to save Pomeroy from an ignominious death upon the scaffold.

The trial excited more than ordinary interest even in murder cases. The courtroom was crowded from day to day and the testimony was carefully noted.

After a jury had been selected District Attorney May delivered the opening argument as follows:

"May it please the Court and you, Gentlemen of the Jury: The prisoner at the bar, Jesse Harding Pomeroy, stands indicted, as you have just heard, for the murder of Horace H. Millen. Murder, gentlemen, according to the definition which formerly prevailed, was an intentional killing of a fellow being. Malice aforethought was and is the first element in murder; but as the experience of men became enlarged and, perhaps, the spirit of Christianity modified somewhat by the civilization of the times it was found that there were degrees of depravity even in murder itself.

Formerly the killing of a man intentionally was considered even in its least aggravated form as justly forfeiting the right of the murderer to live. But a more humane view has been taken of that and the law now, both in this State and in most other civilized communities, has established certain grades even in the crime of murder.

It is obvious, gentlemen, that the man who goes deliberately about the murder of his fellow man for gain, for instance, and uses violent means, discovers a more deliberate malice than the man, who, in a passion, suddenly, though unintentionally, kills his fellow man, after more or less provocation.

In this State, gentlemen, the law has defined murder to be of two degrees: murder committed with deliberately premeditated malice aforethought, or in the commission, or attempt to commit any crime punishable with death, or imprisonment for life, or committed with extreme atrocity or cruelty, is murder in the first degree. Murder not appearing to be in the first degree is murder in the second degree. The degree of murder shall be found by the jury.

According to the view, gentlemen, which the Commonwealth takes of the evidence in this case it will not be necessary for me to detain you a moment with any observations upon the law of homicide under circumstances which reduce the grade below that of murder.

The facts in this case, gentleman, are briefly: that on the second day of April last the body of a boy, an infant I might call him four years and three months old, — three months and a few days, — was found upon the marsh that lies intervening between the promontory of Saven Hill in Dorchester. It is in what is known by those who have lived in that section of the city as 'the Cow Pasture,' a large tract of marsh land lying east of the Old Colony railroad and Dorchester Avenue and stretching away nearly east for a mile to the water. About halfway down that marsh, about two thousand feet in a straight line from Crescent Avenue station on the Old Colony railroad, and but a few feet from the water's edge, the body of this little boy was found, while it was yet warm, with the throat cut, some fifteen or twenty stabs in the region of the heart and mutilated the little boy's hands were also wounded, more or less. — There were marks of wounds upon his arms, suggesting, perhaps, the possibility of feeble struggles to resist. This body was found by another boy, who had been down there, I think, clamming with his brother, and it was found about 3 o'clock, if I remember right. Upon discovering this body the little boy. Powers, looked away up the marsh towards the railroad and saw two men, one of whom had a gun. He immediately went to that man, told him what he had found and requested him to go with him to the place. That man, accompanied by his friend, who was with him, — he had been out shooting at a mark within a very short time there — then accompanied him to the spot and there found what I have already described.

He dispatched messengers hither and thither for police officers and remained there until the police officers came. After the police officers came the body was taken to the Crescent Avenue station, off the marsh, then to Police Station 9 in Roxbury, and thence to the undertaker's.

After an inquest had been held the body was returned to the parents, who meanwhile had been found. The parents of this boy, Millen, had not resided long in South Boston; but a few days, I think, certainly but a few weeks.

On the morning of the day when this boy disappeared he was at play in the neighborhood of his father's, about the steps — there was, I think, a flight of steps on the corner of Eighth Street and Dorchester Avenue — where children were accustomed to go, and he was seen about the steps.

The last that his mother saw of him was about half-past 10 o'clock. She was, I believe, engaged that day in washing, or was quite busy. He had been out to play and would occasionally run up to the house to speak to his mother and then run off. The last time she saw him was about half-past 10 o'clock, when she gave him a penny to go the baker's and buy him a cake. He was seen afterwards between half-past 10 o'clock and half-past 11.

There will be amongst the witnesses some discrepancy as to the time, because the time was not noticed then there being no occasion to notice it carefully. But from half-past 10 to half-past 11 o'clock he was seen in that neighborhood by several people accompanied by a larger boy, whom the government expect the evidence will satisfy you was the defendant at the bar. Subsequently to that time they were seen together on the Old Colony railroad from a quarter to half-a-mile distant from this boy's house — the Millen boy's house — going towards McKay's wharf, which lies just at the edge of this cow pasture, or marsh.

That was not far from 12 o'clock, and not far also from 12 o'clock the two were seen together, apparently having gone down on McKay's wharf, crossed a bridge, which leads from that over the creek to the boat house, which is upon the shore, and jumped off from this bridge on to the marsh. Having jumped off from this bridge upon the marsh they proceeded down till they came to a creek which they passed, or went around, I am not certain which. Then they came to a ditch, when the Pomeroy boy lifted the Millen boy over. At this creek they were met by another boy, who was coming off, who had been down where they were digging clams and was coming off the marsh. Then it was not five minutes from 12 o'clock — just after 12 o'clock.

The Pomeroy boy spoke to this boy, who was coming off, and enquired what the men were shooting down on the marsh. He received a reply and then went on with the Millen boy, leading him by the left hand. As I have said just now, when they came to the ditch he was seen to lift the Millen boy over and set him down. Then they proceeded side by side, down the marsh. He was not seen again by that witness. It will be shown to you, gentlemen that the tracks, which were made both by the Millen boy and by the Pomeroy boy when they jumped from the bridge on to the marsh, correspond exactly to the boots worn by the respective boys.

The body was found some fifty feet, I think, across the creek, half-way down the marsh, on the South Boston side. There were about their many footsteps, because diver's parties had visited the scene; four men and some boys certainly, perhaps five, before any particular examination was made.

Upon a careful examination it was found that at the nearest practicable point of crossing that creek, on returning towards Boston, there were footsteps. We shall show you that similar tracks were found from that point leading towards the point where the body was found, here and there, of course, there being a difference in the impression made according to the varying hardness, or softness, of the marsh, and according as it was covered with sand, or covered with grass, as it was in different places.

There were plain indications of two sets of tracks, large ones and small ones, having the same relations to each other; that is: the small ones were on the left side of the larger, and at diver's points corresponding exactly with the boots which were worn by the respective boys.

There were footsteps, corresponding exactly, upon application being made with the boots which were worn by the Pomeroy boy, and from point to point along the curve of the marsh these tracks could be traced until, forced by another creek he passed around it and crossed the track by which he went down to the place where the body was found.

We shall show you, gentlemen, that a boy corresponding in size and appearance and in dress, so far as those were observed, was seen about 1 o'clock running off the marsh in the direction, which those footprints indicate, towards the Old Colony railroad and frequently looking behind as if pursued.

The Pomeroy boy resided in South Boston, on Broadway, not far from the place where the Millen family resided.

These are the main facts, gentlemen, which the Commonwealth will produce to you upon this line of the prosecution.

The Commonwealth will also introduce to another and a distinct species of evidence. That is confession! And they have been somewhat embarrassed in determining whether they would not rely upon the confession alone without going into the details of a murder attended by such atrocity. But upon the whole it was thought the prudent and the better course to present to you, substantially, everything that was known by the Commonwealth about the matter. And it is with that view that I have detailed to you the evidence which the Commonwealth believes will satisfy you that Horace H. Millen was murdered by Jesse Harding Pomeroy.

You will now see, gentlemen, the reason why I did not feel it my duty to address you at all upon the grade of homicide less than murder. The Commonwealth cannot conceive that there can be any doubt that, whatever else may be thought about this transaction, there can be no doubt that it was a murder with deliberately premeditated malice aforethought; and that it was a murder attended by such circumstances of atrocity and cruelty as to bring it unquestionably within the definition of the statute constituting murder in the first degree.

My duty, gentlemen, is substantially performed, having thus stated to you the facts which the Commonwealth expect to prove and the law upon which they rest their case.

I know, gentlemen that I need not say that you occupy a responsible position. I know I need not say to you that the safety and the stability of society practically rests in your hands.

Every one of us has yielded his right of personal and private vengeance to the society, which has taken that right in trust and which has promised to protect all from the unlawful acts of such members of society as may not be restrained and controlled by law.

And it is because that right has been yielded that we live in a community, where life and property are regarded as safe, since the tribunals have been of such a character that they have discharged fearlessly their duty in the protection of the public.

I shall not, gentlemen, take up your time with any other observations. The Commonwealth has no interest in stimulating you to do anything which is not necessary for the public safety.

The Commonwealth can have no possible object in the conviction of an innocent person; but the Commonwealth, represented here by its prosecuting officers, is bound to carry out in good faith, for the protection of the innocent and the law-abiding, the trust which is imposed upon them, and which they have accepted, of protecting those who have yielded their own right of self-defence."

CHAPTER V.
THE MOST REMARKABLE CASE IN THE HISTORY OF CRIME OR CRIMINAL LAW.

HON. CHARLES ROBINSON, JR., made the opening argument for the defence.

In addressing the jury he said he feared "that Jesse did kill the boy."

He stated that the crime was committed April 22, 1874, and that Jesse at that time was fourteen years and five months old. "An age," said the counsel "when, the law says, he can be held for the crime. It is the most remarkable case in the history of crime, or criminal law."

The lawyer proceeded and stated that at one time Jesse ill-treated a cat which was seen to run away from him, with eyes glaring, showing that it had been in pain.

In the Winthrop school, in Charlestown, in 1871, he made faces in school. The teacher said that at times it was utterly impossible to make him understand. When reprimanded he would say, 'I could not help it.' He thought it very unjust if he was punished.

Continuing, Mr. Robinson said: "After that, I think, in December. 1871, was the first time that this boy departed from

anything so very unusual when he commenced a career, which is certainly unknown before; unparalleled, I think, in the treatment of other boys. Undoubtedly you may have heard of it.

I propose to put in the facts in the case as they came to my knowledge.

I find that as early as December 1871, while he was living in Charlestown, he goes over to Chelsea and takes a strange boy with him up to the top of Powder Horn Hill, some two or three miles from where this boy lived, and entirely out of his duty, calling or business, took the boy up there, a stranger, and strips the young child, I think that follows in every case, whips the child somewhat, and made him go through certain acts before him and then told him to go home.

In February 1872, another act of this kind occurred. The boy goes from his home, unknown to his parents, and finds a boy over in Chelsea, a stranger to him, and takes him up to the top of Powder Horn Hill and there goes through similar actions with him. I think that was in the winter, he was put up there in some ice. He whipped the boy some and stuck some pins in him and went through a general performance.

I cannot detail each one to you.

Here in July, again, he took another boy, a Chelsea boy, he still living in Charlestown; for he went from Charlestown to Chelsea; he did not seem to go to any other place. He took that boy up to Powder Horn Hill and went through the same series with him. I do not mean to say precisely the same things, but substantially; whipping the boy more or less, taking off his clothes and making him get upon a stone and dance. In one instance he made the boy say 'the Lord's Prayer.'

Here were three of them at Chelsea. About the first of August the family removed to South Boston. He had been there but a short time before he commenced the same thing there with the boys, who were utter strangers.

On the 17th day of August he took a strange boy out near these marshes, where the Millen boy was killed, and there he goes through the same performances with this boy; whips him, strips him and makes him say things and dances around him.

The next transaction was on the 8th day of September 1872, when he takes another boy. He whipped them all and made them take off their clothes and went through these various performances.

On September 11, three days afterwards, he took another one of these boys, who were utter strangers to him, and he to them, out near the same place on the marsh. The four South Boston boys all went out to the marsh. He went through the same performance and took out a large knife which he seemed to have carried in a pocket in his coat. I understand it was a sort of old butcher's knife, which was used about the house, or was used for carving. This boy was the first one that was cut seriously. He was cut on the head. I have the boy here. As I understand he danced around him, and while the blood was on the knife and running from it, he sat and laughed to see the blood dripping-off.

Again, on the 17th six days afterwards, he takes another boy, an entire stranger, out and ties him down to a telegraph post, near the bridge there, out in that vicinity and whipped him some.

These matters, of course, you will, probably, remember, as I do, were more or less exciting to the community as to who was causing these acts. Subsequently, on the 20th day of September, he was arrested as the party who was troubling the children.

The counsel stated that he pleaded guilty and was sent to the State Reform School. There was no proof against him except the statements of small boys. There was some doubt of his guilt in the community.

At the Reform School he attempted to use a knife but was discovered by a teacher.

When discovered he said he was not going to do anything. At one time a snake was killed in the road. When Jesse saw the blood, he seemed to want to kill the snake again. It was with great difficulty that he was got away.

After that he behaved well and was discharged from the school. He said he would never do a wrong thing again" The counsel continued: "The first transaction after he came out, which I shall put in proof, is a transaction prior in date to this murder. This transaction occurred on the 22d day of April. On the 8th day of March, I understand, he did on that day kill the Curran girl and under circumstances like these:

That Jesse, by his mother's request or general direction, went to open her store. She kept a small place, being a dressmaker and supporting the family by means of a store and her labor. She sent him there to open the store. He had another brother, an elder brother, who sold papers. He went there at half-past S o'clock in the morning to open this store and while he was there engaged in sweeping it out the Curran girl came in. She was an entire stranger to him and him to her and before her coming in there he did not know there was a Curran girl in the world. She came in by direction of her mother to purchase an article of some kind.

Instantly the thought came to him and he told her to go into the cellar, and then within three minutes from the time the girl went into that cellar, or store, she was dead! She went and asked for some article. He told her it was down stairs. She went down and he immediately locked the front door. As I understand, she stepped down and stood right in the centre of the place below, facing Broadway.

He stepped up behind her and in an instant cut her throat.

It was done in an instant!

She died quite suddenly, without any great struggle.

He then took her and drew her on one side and covered her over with some few things and left her. She was missed, but no suspicion was aroused as to where she was and no tidings could be got where she went to.

The next transaction was this transaction, of which you have heard today. These are the particular transactions connected with this boy.

I understand the boy to say, since these matters came out, that he cannot control himself; that if he was out, that is, if he was at liberty, he might do nothing, yet, on the other hand, if the opportunity arose he could not resist even if it was your boy or mine. As I once put the question: —

'If it was my little boy and I should leave him would he be safe?'

He said, 'No.'

He should not mean to do anything, but it did not make any odds whose boy it was. If this feeling came up, which he cannot control, and which, he says, is irresistible, he would do these things again.

Those are the acts with which the boy has been connected, something exceedingly remarkable.

From the evidence that I get in the case and what I shall be able to offer to you, I think that I shall satisfy you that this boy has an original defect, or want of capacity; that there is something wanting in him. Has always been something wanting in him, and that there is not a power in him by which he can control his actions, or control these impulses, when these impulses come over him.

I have not been able to ascertain any motive why he does these acts. I have failed yet to discover any motive. I propose to put all these facts in regard to this boy before you and present this case with a full statement upon every fact bearing and touching upon this boy because I feel like this: I feel that in one respect this boy cannot go out safely. We all feel that it would not be safe to the community to have him at large.

In my neighborhood, where I have my children, I would move, because there is no more safety with that boy around than there is with powder and tire in close proximity. Therefore I have got this offer: I shall offer some evidence about these peculiarities. I think there is an original want of capacity. I also think there is evidenced here that there is a sort of mental disease, which affects him, and that these acts are the acts of disease as well as of an original want of capacity, and that upon no other theory can you intelligently account for his case.

Gentlemen: you perceive that there are some nine instances, seven instances of cutting and torturing boys; a confinement of sixteen months in the State Reform School; a discharge from -there; and then a little more than two months from the time of his discharge from the State Reform School he kills two children. As I understand the case, if he had had an opportunity within the last six months he might have killed six more.

Now, upon that matter, of course, you will understand by what I have said the view I take of the case. I take this view of the case: that this boy has not the capacity, either by a want of having it originally, or by being born with evil powers, or by reason of disease, he is not a being responsible. In other words it comes within the language of the statute that he is an insane person and insanity may be there. It is a term which is broad, the term insanity; yet the statute has defined it as follows:

'The word insane person, or lunatic, shall include every idiot, non-compos, or insane, distracted person.'

I suppose I may also say that the term insane means also a person who is of unsound mind. That if he is deficient in that power by which he is able to control himself; if he has not the power to withstand. This boy understands what is wrong and what is right. He understands, sometimes, if he does an act that he is liable to be punished for it. And yet, notwithstanding this, and although he was in school and learned somewhat rapidly; and from the statement, which he wrote and which was read; he has some capacity in that direction.

Nevertheless there is this element in him, by which he cannot control himself at certain times, therefore, I shall present this case to you as an act committed by him; by a being, who was not responsible at the time, and, then, if he was not responsible at the time, he is not within the statute, which I read, guilty of murder in the first or second degree; but that he is a person who is not guilty by reason of insanity.

The legislature has passed a law to meet just such a case. — The law reads: "When a person indicted for murder, or manslaughter, is acquitted by the jury by reason of insanity the court shall order such person to be committed to one of the State Lunatic hospitals during his natural life/ I take it that this boy is of this class and upon the evidence which I shall present to you when I come to present my view of the matter, after hearing the evidence, to take that view of the case. The law provides then how this boy shall be taken care of and where he shall have restraint.

I believe I have stated the facts in this matter and all that is necessary is to call my witnesses to give their evidence."

CHAPTER VI.
THE TRIAL RESULTS IN THE CONVICTION OF POMEROY OF MURDER IN THE FIRST DEGREE.

AS WOULD NATURALLY BE EXPECTED there was a large number of witnesses examined during the trial.

The statements made by the District Attorney in his opening argument were corroborated by witnesses so that, notwithstanding the admissions made by the counsel for the defence, the government presented to the jury its case in full.

The defence did not attempt to show that Pomeroy was not the person who had brutally murdered the Millen boy, but endeavored to show that the defendant was not responsible for his acts, as indicated in the able argument of Mr. Robinson given in the preceding chapter. Perhaps the most interesting witness was Mrs. Pomeroy, the mother of the prisoner who testified that the defendant was born on Nov. 29, 1859, in Charlestown. She stated that three or four months after his birth he had a disease of the skin and that there was an ulcer on one of his eyes.

She said he had strange dreams, which he honestly believed were actual facts.

He attended a Sunday school at a mission in Charlestown, presided over by Rev. Mr. Barnard.

She said that Jesse often read the Scriptures to her.

She stated that Jesse had been an inmate of the Reform School and that she worked hard to get him released. She was very glad when it was accomplished. She said Jesse was a bright scholar. Among the other witnesses, who testified, were the police who were interested in the arrest of Pomeroy, and medical experts on the subject of insanity.

As there always has been, and, doubtless, always will be, a decided difference of opinion on the question of insanity, in criminal trials especially, I have omitted giving a lengthy report of such testimony in this case.

When one considers the fact that not a few medical men of repute believe that crime of all grades is the result of insanity, it can be readily seen that there was not wanting in Pomeroy's case evidence tending to show that he was not responsible for his acts.

The evidence being all in, then came the closing arguments.

Mr. Robinson spoke for the prisoner, claiming that insanity had been proven.

Hon. Charles R. Train, attorney general of Massachusetts, made the argument for the government, stating that their case had been made out in every particular.

Chief Justice Gray delivered the charge to the jury.

When the jury returned the foreman stated, in answer to the customary questions, that a verdict had been agreed upon and that the prisoner had been found guilty of murder in the first degree.

Jesse was apparently unmoved when he heard the foreman announce the verdict.

Chief Justice Gray stated that he had received two documents from the jury; one, recounting the atrocity of the crime, and the other, recommending that the sentence be commuted to life imprisonment.

Exceptions were filed by Mr. Robinson and argued by him. They were opposed by Attorney General Train.

The exceptions were that Pomeroy was insane and that certain medical witnesses had not been allowed to be fully heard.

The court took the matter under consideration.

The court finally overruled the exceptions.

The counsel for the condemned boy did not stop in his efforts to save him from death upon the scaffold. Mr. Robinson said, "I must save the life of that boy."

There was no doubt that he firmly believed that Pomeroy was insane.

The next step taken in behalf of the condemned was an appeal to His Excellency, the Governor of the Commonwealth of Massachusetts. Hon. William Gaston occupied that position at the time. The last of March 1875, a hearing was held before the Governor and Council.

Mr. Robinson asked that the sentence of death be commuted to imprisonment for life.

The prosecution was strongly opposed to such action and called for the execution of Pomeroy in accordance with law.

No definite action was taken by the Governor and Council at the time.

Interest in Pomeroy continued unabated and resulted in a public hearing being called before the Governor and Council.

This meeting was held about the middle of April 1875. Governor Gaston and the full Council were present.

A numerously signed petition was presented, asking that executive clemency be extended to Pomeroy.

The petitioners were represented by Hon. Charles Robinson, Jr., and Rev. W.H.H. Murray. The remonstrates were represented by Mr. Paul West.

Dr. Norton Folsom, superintendent of the Massachusetts hospital, and Dr. Walker, superintendent of the South Boston Insane Asylum, stated that they believed that Pomeroy was morally and mentally insane.

Judge Dwight Foster expressed the opinion that the wretched boy should be kept in close confinement for life. "He came into this world," said the Judge, 'with a propensity to commit terrible acts and he should not be put out of it by the gravest act of law.'

Judge Thomas said the boy was born with a congenital weakness and was not morally responsible for his acts. He also said that Pomeroy was a dangerous person and should not be at large.

Rev. Mr. Murray strongly urged the granting of the request of the petitioners.

Mr. West presented a petition in opposition to a commutation of sentence.

Col. Henry H. Wilson spoke in behalf of the ladies, who had signed the remonstrance. He said "I see nothing that calls for mercy in this case, but only a piling up of barbarous crimes, which should not be mistaken for symptoms of insanity."

Mr. Robinson closed the hearing, speaking at length on the mental condition of his client.

The Governor and Council again took the subject under consideration. Meanwhile Pomeroy remained an inmate of the Charles Street jail in Boston.

The Governor would not issue the death warrant, and, consequently, the execution could not take place.

The much discussed question of what to do with the murderer remained undecided until Sept. 2, 1876, when Governor Rice, who had succeeded Governor Gaston, and his council, by a vote of six to three, commuted Pomeroy's sentence to close confinement for life in the Massachusetts State Prison.

This was the first and only vote taken by the Council. The reason given by the majority for their action was the recommendation of the Pomeroy jury.

Soon after decided action had been taken in this case the law was changed in regard to executions in Massachusetts making it obligatory upon the Court, and not the Governor, to set the time of death of a condemned criminal.

There was more or less feeling concerning the action of Governor Rice and Council in regard to Pomeroy. "Why should Governor Rice hang Pomeroy when Governor Gaston would not do it?" was asked by Governor Rice's friends of those opposed to the commutation of the sentence of the boy fiend.

The editor of the South Boston Inquirer expressed the feelings of many residents of that section when he wrote: "The community is disappointed with the result and we presume the whole State will be. There is no safety for the people while such a monster lives, even if he is confined; escape is possible; pardon is probable in a few years. It is well the charge of murder of Katie Curran still remains as a final resort in case he is pardoned."

Pomeroy entered the prison soon after the commutation of his sentence.

CHAPTER VII.

POMEROY'S NUMEROUS, BUT UNSUCCESSFUL ATTEMPTS TO ESCAPE FROM CONFINEMENT.

FROM THE TIME WHEN Jesse was locked up in jail until the present day his greatest desire has been to effect an escape.

Like a bird in a cage, he has been continually in search for some weak spot in his room by means of which he might gain his liberty.

No one can conscientious blame Pomeroy for this for the reason that in the first place death stared him in the face. And secondly, after the commutation of his sentence, there was before him a life of imprisonment.

By attempting to make an escape he has had everything to gain and not anything to lose. If detected in his efforts to obtain his liberty, there could be but little additional punishment inflicted upon him. He was suffering the most severe punishment the State could give him. He was living in what might be termed a tomb!

It was with the idea that he would cheat the gallows that he attempted to effect an escape from the Charles Street jail while awaiting the disposition of his case.

The discovery of this attempt was made on Tuesday, July 20, 1875.

With the aid of a piece of wire, broken from his tin basin, he began digging out the mortar in his cell. So well did he plan the work that, but for a timely discovery, he would have been able in a few hours to have got into the corridor. Once outside his cell it was his intention, it was said, to knock down, or even kill, any person, who stood in his way.

He next made a study of a window, recently put in. He wrote to friends, with the idea of attempting to make an escape, to bring him a file concealed in a banana. He said he wanted to go to Canada!

Letters of this character were found and laid before the Governor and Council.

After Jesse had been committed to the Massachusetts State Prison at Charlestown, he began to cause trouble for the officers. At the same time some of his relatives appeared to be very anxious concerning him. They often expressed fears that he was being harshly treated. This, however, was very far from being the fact.

It was sometime in the year 1887; I think it was in the Spring; when a relative of the convict urged that something be done for Jesse, who was suffering from an ingrown nail on the big toe of the right foot. General Chamberlain, then warden of the prison, said that Pomeroy should be properly attended to in that particular.

Dr. Latimer was the prison physician. He made an examination of the toe and concluded that the nail would have to be removed. It was decided to perform the operation on a Sabbath morning when everything about the institution would be more than ordinarily quiet.

When relatives of Pomeroy ascertained what was to be done, some of them asked the warden to be allowed to be present when the nail was removed. This request was refused, but the warden told them not to worry as he would be present during the operation.

One beautiful Sabbath morning, while services were being held in the chapel, Jesse was brought from his room in the upper arch to the hospital. He was then laid on the operating board and Warden Chamberlain, who was in the chapel at the time, was summoned.

Jesse lay on his back on the board and when the Warden came beside him he said:

"Good morning, Warden."

"Good morning, Jesse," said the Warden. "How do you feel today?"

"I feel very happy today," replied the convict. "I had a very pleasant dream last night.

"Indeed." remarked the Warden.

"Yes, sir. I dreamed that I was free," continued Jesse, his face brightening up, "free to go where I wished and no one to stop me. Oh! How beautiful the grass, and trees, and flowers seemed to me. I ran about. I rolled in the grass. I was so happy. And then I awoke only to think over what I had been dreaming. Warden, do you think I shall ever be free?"

There was a peculiar smile on Pomeroy's face when he said this.

"I cannot answer that question," was the answer made by the Warden.

At this point the convict was put under the influence of ether and the operation was quickly and successfully performed. I have never heard of Jesse making a complaint concerning his big toe since that day.

The next Sabbath there was great excitement at the prison. The occasion of it was that Pomeroy had made an attempt to escape.

He was confined, as I have said, in a room in the upper arch, which next to the lower arch, or dungeon, was considered the most secure part of the prison. With the exception of the door which was of iron, the room was built of heavy blocks of granite. Pomeroy had succeeded in removing the cement around one of these blocks with the intention of pushing it out into the yard and to leave his room through the aperture.

If he had succeeded in getting out of his cell, he would then have been in the yard, surrounded by a high wall which he must have scaled in order to have obtained his freedom.

He had partially pushed out the block of granite he had been at work upon. It protruded so far that it was noticed by one of the yard officers, who reported the fact to the Warden.

An examination of the cell was immediately made and the facts I have mentioned were brought to light.

Pomeroy was removed to another room while the one that he had occupied was repaired.

He made no reply when asked why he had attempted to make an escape.

In a short time Pomeroy was returned to his old room and resumed his work of brush making.

At that time the convicts were employed by contractors, Pomeroy was in the brush department and had become a very good and rapid workman.

It was not long after his attempted escape that Pomeroy and all the other convicts were removed from Charlestown to the new prison at Concord, Mass.

Jesse was given a room, which was considered one of the strongest in the prison, he being still kept in close confinement. As soon as he was put in the room, he began an investigation to ascertain if he could effect an escape.

The result was that Jesse worried the officers a great deal. On three occasions he nearly succeeded in getting out of his room. He cut through wood work and also removed the steel bars to his windows. This was done at each of the three attempts.

Fearing that he might succeed the Warden caused Pomeroy's room to be covered with boiler iron. It would hardly seem possible that thus enclosed that a prisoner could hope to escape.

Jesse was not discouraged. He seemed to think that the greater the obstacle the more he should exert himself.

After the boiler iron had been put in, he made several attempts to escape. He cut off the heads of the bolts, which held the plates together. He always tried to get at a window.

Vigilance on the part of the officers, more than the strength of the prison, prevented Pomeroy from escaping.

Concord prison was far from being strong. This was shown by the fact that a convict, put in a punishment cell at 10 o'clock in the forenoon, was at 1 o'clock, the same day captured in the yard. He had removed a portion of a window frame, and, becoming possessed of an iron weight, had broken through the brick wall.

I was told that Pomeroy suddenly desisted from attempting to escape on account of an order given the officers to shoot him if he should be found in the yard. I will not vouch for the truth of the report.

A revolt and a series of exciting scenes at the Concord prison had the effect, not only of awakening a renewed interest in prison matters, but caused the return of the convicts to the old bastille of the Commonwealth of Massachusetts in Charlestown.

Pomeroy was again placed in close confinement in the upper arch.

Soon after his return to Charlestown he began to make plans for an escape. He frequently cut the bars of the door of his room.

In a short time the iron bars of his cell door were removed and steel bars substituted. It was thought that no farther trouble, at least for some time, would be caused by the determined prisoner.

In this regard the management was mistaken and greatly surprised.

On Thursday, Nov. 10, 1887, the officers and inmates of the prison were startled by the noise made by an explosion. An investigation showed that Pomeroy had been tampering with a gas pipe, which was around the outside of his cell.

With the aid of a knife blade, which he had made into a saw, he removed the cement from between a number of the granite blocks comprising the walls of his cell, and had also sawn the gas pipe. To this pipe he attached a pipe of his own manufacture, made of cloth and paper, which he had pasted together. The cement he took from the wall he put in a pail in such small quantities that it was not detected.

He placed his bed blanket over the pipe before he lighted the gas. It was a wonder he was not killed. As it was his eyes were injured. Had he not had the best of treatment at the hands of Dr. Sawin there is but little doubt that he would have become blind.

The explosion tore off the plastering in the hospital, rent the walls of the upper arch in several places and did other damage. No one appeared to know where the convict obtained the tools he worked with, except that he made some of them out of articles furnished by the prison.

Pomeroy was sent to the hospital, his cell was repaired and in time he was returned to his old room.

Notwithstanding repeated defeats he continued to cut the bolts and bars of his cell door. On two occasions he succeeded in getting out of his room and was found roaming about the upper arch.

By authority of the legislature of Massachusetts an addition 75 was made to the hospital wing of the prison, the upper arch being under the hospital. This resulted in a special room being built for Pomeroy. It was as strong as it was possible to make a cell.

The convict, however, continued to cut bars and tamper with locks.

CHAPTER VIII.
THE MANNER IN WHICH THE CONVICT PASSES HIS HOURS. — "A CHILD OF THE DEVIL."

FOR SIXTEEN YEARS JESSE has been an inmate of the Massachusetts State Prison. During all of those years he has been in close confinement. With the exception of his frequent attempts to escape he has been a good prisoner. That is: he has not committed an assault, or harmed any person.

During a number of years, under the contract system, he was employed by a brush company and worked diligently. His workshop was his cell. His mind was fully occupied.

In moments when not asleep, or at work, he read considerably. One of his favorite books was "The Life of Napoleon." He was especially interested in the life of the great general on St. Helena. There were many other books which he read, as there is a line library in the prison. He also began the study of arithmetic and grammar, but never made much progress.

There is no truth in the statements that he is proficient in Greek, or any other language.

As I have stated, his health has been good, although he had. "la grippe"[1] in 1891. The fact that he has been healthy has been due, doubtless, to the regularity of his diet. It may be interesting to the reader to know what the bill of fare at the Massachusetts State Prison comprises. The following is a copy:

SUNDAY.
Breakfast. — Rice and milk, white bread and coffee.
Dinner. — Baked fish or baked meat, white bread, fruit, tea.

MONDAY.
Breakfast. — Oatmeal and milk, white bread and coffee.
Dinner. — Baked beans and brown bread.
Supper. — White bread and tea.

TUESDAY.
Breakfast. — Meat hash, white bread and coffee.
Dinner. — Corned beef and vegetables.
Supper. — Corned beef, white bread and tea.

WEDNESDAY.
Breakfast. — Rice and milk, white bread and coffee.
Dinner. — Beef soup, potatoes and white bread.
Supper. — White bread and tea.

THURSDAY.
Breakfast. — Meat hash, white bread and coffee.
Dinner. — Baked beans and brown bread.
Supper. - Corned beef, white bread and tea.

FRIDAY.
Breakfast. — Mush and milk, white bread and coffee.
Dinner. — Clam chowder, potatoes and white bread.
Supper. — White bread and tea.

---

1. influenza

SATURDAY.

Breakfast. — Meat hash, white bread and coffee.

Dinner. — Beef soup, potatoes and white bread.

Supper. — Corned beef, white bread and tea.

The menu is varied somewhat by the- Warden, who, upon holidays and at other times, at his discretion, introduces articles not named in the bill of fare.

At stated times Jesse has been allowed to receive visits from relatives which have been a source of great pleasure to him. Once a year, perhaps, the Governor and members of the Executive Council visit Pomeroy's cell.

The convict, as a rule, has not been communicative. He has been inclined to be sulky and when questioned has made brief and evasive answers. When, however, he has desired to make an impression in his own favor he has been very talkative.

Since the abolition of the contract system in the penal institutions of Massachusetts Pomeroy's hours have passed slowly. All he has had to do has been to eat, read, sleep and walk about his room. Occasionally he has been given outdoor exercise in the yard, but always accompanied by an officer. Sounds from the outside world rarely reach his ears. The upper arch has always been as silent as the grave.

Thus has the convict lived year after year, without anything to hope for except a pardon, or effecting an escape. And yet his life has ever been dear to him.

Nearly every person, who has visited the Massachusetts State Prison, has asked about Pomeroy and expressed a desire to see him. Under no circumstances have visitors been allowed to enter the upper arch. Occasionally permission has been given visitors to look through a small aperture in a heavy iron door, but all that could be seen was a row of cells. Not a human being was in sight.

In all probability Pomeroy will die in prison. With the terrible record which he has no executive would have the temerity to pardon him. Only by the grossest negligence could he effect an escape.

It is generally admitted that Jesse was born with evil propensities. As a number of horrible crimes have recently been committed, not only in the United States, but in Europe, attributable to such conditions, attention has been attracted to the subject. Distinguished medical men, who have made a study of the matter, claim that disease of such a character can be cured. The statement has not been well received by individuals, who have had more or less to do with criminals. The Somerville boy, who murdered his employer, George Codman, a milk dealer, and scattered the severed remains in the snow along Lexington roads, was said to be a victim of heredity. No one appeared to have known this until after the crime had been committed. No one can truthfully deny the progressiveness of science, and yet there have been individuals who have not believed it possible for science to accurately determine whether or not a man would become a criminal.

CHAPTER IX.
A GLANCE AT POMEROY'S YOUTH. — JESSE'S UNACCOUNTABLE DEPRAVITY.

IN MY SEARCH FOR FACTS concerning Pomeroy I found in the Boston Globe an article relating incidents of his youth. I made the following quotations:

"As I remember Jesse, he was a couple of years older than I, and the quietest and most retiring boy I ever knew. He seldom had a word to say for himself or anybody else. He would never kick the football with the other boys, but sit on a fence or stone wall and overlook the job. When it came to choosing up sides for a terrific game of baseball, Jesse would never consent to be on either side — nor would he umpire the game.

If we coaxed real hard, he would keep the score, sitting on the green, with his eyes cast down, and sticking his knife into the sod, absently, not at all viciously. When it came to swimming and jumping off crosstrees of schooners and coal stagings into the bay, Jesse was not in it. He would sit on the wharf or on the side of the schooner, legs dangling over, quiet and furtive.

If we made a night raid on Dr. Howe's orchard, Jesse wouldn't be with us. Often, on Sundays, we would hire a boat at old City Point, at a quarter of a dollar an hour, and go rowing across too far away orchards. Jesse would sit in the bow or stern and let us pull at the oars. That was remarkable, for we all wanted to row.

Jesse was the only boy I ever knew who wouldn't try to pull a boat out of the water with an oar."

"One fine day there came into the school-room, in which Jesse had a seat and desk, the headmaster, a Mr. Barnes, I think, an officer and one of the unknown's victims. The little fellow had been found, I think, in Chelsea, hung up and cut up. When he recovered, he said it wasn't a man with red whiskers and hair who had treated him so, but a boy who looked to be four or live years older than himself. In fact, 'like a school-boy,' he said. So they took this poor little muti- lated chap around to all the schools in Boston, I believe, until they came to, I think, the Bigelow school.

'Do you see him here?' said the master to the little victim.

'N-no,' hesitatingly replied the little fellow. Then, sharply, from the lady teacher: 'Pomeroy! Why don't you hold up your head?'

Slowly Jesse raised his head. And the boy screamed: 'That's him! That's him! I'd know him by his eye!'

And so Jesse was arrested, tried, found guilty and sentenced to the Westboro Reform School. If Jesse had been ill that day — ill enough to have kept himself in the house — he might be rivaling Jack the Ripper now.

Jesse had a bad eye. Not in a wicked sense, but we boys used to say that Jesse had a lace curtain over his eye. It was a white eye; his other eye was a mild, I think, blue one. I always felt sorry for him on account of the sad, sort of appealing, dog like look in those eyes of his. As I remember him, he had light brown hair, and was always neatly dressed.

Jesse never quarreled with or raised his voice to anyone. His manners were perfect. But he had a hard time of it in the Westboro Reform School. The boys there—the majority of them—were in for playing truant and being unmanageably wild. Jesse was treat- ed as a common pickpocket would be by burglars.

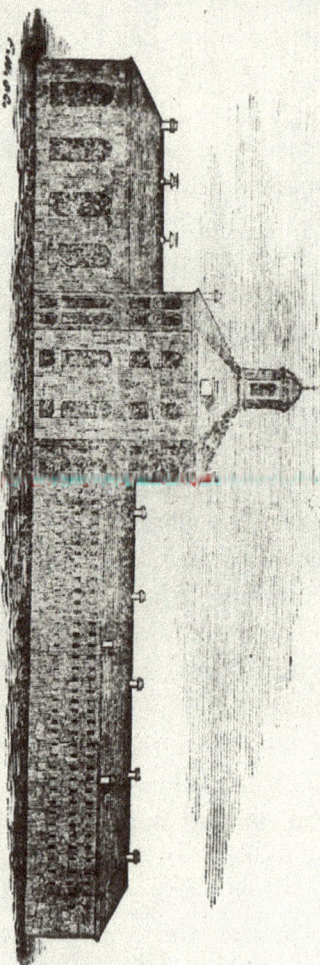

MASSACHUSETTS STATE PRISON AT CHARLESTOWN.

EAST FRONT ELEVATION OF DORMITORY BUILDING OF 1826, AND EXTENSION OF 1850, INCLUDING CENTRE BUILDING AND SOUTH WING.

There are several grades even in boy's prisons, and scavengers cannot mingle with aristocrats. So every time a boy got a chance Jesse was whipped. His story had got over the school. But his mother bent all her energies toward his release, with the result that Jesse was liberated to read novels behind his brother's newsstand, for he was shunned by the boys in the fields.

He was out a little while when I met him one day while I was going on skates under full sail down the bay to Fort Independence. All we had to do in those days was to open our jackets, face the south, and the wind would do the rest for miles. He was coming up afoot, striking at a wooden block with a 'hockey.' I cried out 'Hello, Jesse!' but he didn't take any notice of me.

Sometimes we wouldn't see Jesse for days and days. — Then suddenly, he would slope onto our playground with a shoulder shrug by way of reply to our salutations, and get away by; by himself to resume his old occupation of sticking his knife into the green sward.

The only time that Jesse would brighten up was when we -played; 'Scouts and Indians.' I always insisted on playing Wild Bill, because he had killed thirty-nine men, and Buffalo Bill, Dashing Charlie Emmett, Texas Jack, Wrestling Joe and Squirrell Cap were each impersonated by a competent artist. The Indians were entrusted to boys who expected to get thrashed, and who generally deserved nothing but a thrashing.

Jesse would watch us, but he thought it unfair that the Indians were always wiped out, while the scouts were victorious, he seemed to think more of the Indians than he did of the scouts. I guess that was because he was such a novel reader. He always had a brick-colored 'Beadle' or a white-covered 'Munro' in his pocket or hand. In school he used to keep a novel back of his history, grammar or geography, and devour it while pretending to study his lessons.

Simon Gerty, I remember, was his hero, while the rest of us swore by Kenton, Boone and the Wetzels. Jesse used to think that it was a fine thing to be a renegade like Gerty; to be the one white man in a great Indian tribe like the Shawnees; to have lots of squaws to do all the work, while he sat around and discussed roasted venison.

Then the fun with the prisoners of war! The running of the gauntlet, and the different modes of putting captives to death.

It was all wildly extravagant talk and not worth writing about but for the fact that at that very time Boston was in a sea. Of excitement over the outrages perpetrated by some unknown person on little boys from 8 to 9 years of age.

One week the news would come that a little boy was found tied to a telegraph pole on the Old Colony or Boston, Hartford and Erie road, horribly mutilated, with his back in ribbons and caked with salt. The next week or month another little boy, (it was never a boy of Jesse's size or age, nor anywhere near it,) would be found in Chelsea, or East Boston, or Jamaica Plain, or Dorchester, mutilated and cut in the same way. Sometimes a boy was found tied to a tree, sometimes in an old barn, but oftener to a telegraph pole on some railroad. Fathers began to tell their boys to be careful of 'a man with red hair and beard,' as the Goth was described by his victims, and mothers were anxious if their boys were out of their sight for half-a-day.

We used to talk about this earlier 'Ripper' among ourselves, but Jesse never had anything to say about it, one way or the other. Then the number of boys who were 'chased,' and escaped by the enamel of their teeth, at about this time, was legion."

In looking over the files of the Chelsea Pioneer and Telegraph, back in the seventies, I found an article, entitled "Unaccountable Depravity." It was as follows:

"Some months ago a big boy decoyed a smaller one to an old house in the rear of Powder Horn Hill, where he stripped and tied, and beat him in a most cruel manner without any provocation, or apparent motive, whatever. This fiendish brute has appeared again, for it can hardly be possible that the same vileness should have an imitator.

On Monday last, about 10 o'clock, a little boy, eight years old, named John Balch, was gazing wistfully into Tolley's toy store on Park street, when he was accosted by a large boy, 10 or

17 years of age, who asked the little lad if he did not wish to make a quarter of a dollar. The lad replied in the affirmative.

'Then come with me,' he said. 'I will show you the man — he wants you to carry a small bundle — to do an errand.'

And the two boys went off together.

When about half-way the Balch boy began to demur.

His evil genius encouraged him to proceed. The distance, he said, was not much further, and the man was waiting to give him the 25 cents, and so on, until they reached the spot back of Powder Horn, near the brick kiln.

Here the villain enticed him into an old house when he threatened the boy if he made the least outcry he would kill him.

He stripped off the boy's clothes, gagged him by stuffing a handkerchief in his mouth, tied him up by the wrists to a beam, with cords which he had brought for the purpose, and hogged him with a rope unmercifully and fiendishly.

When the boy asked why he did so, his reply was, 'the man told me to do it.'

When he had whipped the poor victim about ten minutes, till he was black and blue, he added a few severe kicks, and being apparently satisfied with his cords in Ills pocket, telling place he would kill him.

The boy afraid to go out and sat there till someone came in.

Meantime the parents, who live in the Academy of Music building, and who are newcomers to the city, missed their son and looked for him till evening, fearing he might have fallen off one of the wharves.

They were surprised to see him returning about 5 o'clock. He had been absent from 10 to 5.

The boy can identify the fiend when he sees him.

The City Council has offered a reward of $500 for his conviction."

This brings to a close the history of Massachusetts' most noted criminal.

Belle Sorenson Gunness

(November 11, 1859–April 28, 1908?)

SHE WAS A NORWEGIAN AMERICAN SERIAL KILLER. Most of her victims were her suitors, boyfriends, and all her children. Her motives were life insurance, money, and getting rid of witnesses. She was never apprehended.

Gunness was born in Christiania, Norway. Her father, Peter Paulsen, was a traveling conjurer and a magician; Belle took part in the shows by dancing on a tightrope. Because of the successful business, her father retired and bought a farm in their native land.

In the early 1880s, Belle came to the United States. Two years after being there, she married a Swedish man named Albert Sorenson, and they lived in Chicago. In 1900, Albert Sorenson died under suspicious circumstances from apparent heart failure, but his relatives believed he was poisoned. As a result of his death, Belle got $8,500 from his life insurance.

Belle then moved to Austin, Illinois and shortly after, her home burned down. With no proof of fraud, the insurance company had to pay her. After this, she went back to Chicago where she started a confectionary store which was destroyed by a fire. This time, there was an investigation, but the insurance officials were forced to pay her.

Not long after, she bought a farm about six miles from La Porte, Indiana and married Peter Gunness. A week after marriage, Peter's infant daughter died of uncertain causes while in Belle's care. It's unclear why Belle killed her. A few months later, she killed Peter for insurance money. She told everyone part of a sausage grinder machine fell from a high shelf causing a fatal head injury. Belle's foster daughter, Jennie Olson, told a classmate that Belle had killed her father. Soon after, Jennie disappeared. According to Belle, she went to Lutheran College in Los Angeles. She was never seen alive again.

It is believed Belle killed a total of 25-40 people. When her house burned down in 1908, the skeletons of her children were found, and among them another skeleton the townspeople thought to be Belle's. At the time, investigators couldn't prove the skeleton belonged to her. To this day, some believe that she had faked her own death and escaped.

TIMELINE

1859   -On Nov 11, Belle Gunness is born

1880s   -Belle comes to the US and suspicious deaths start happening on April 25

1884   -Her house burns down and she gets insurance money
-Her first husband dies and she claims his two life insurance policies

1902   -In April, Belle marries Peter Gunness
-A week after being married, Peter's infant daughter dies
-In December, Peter has a fatal 'accident'
-Jennie Olson, her oldest foster daughter, tells a classmate her mother killed her father

1903   -Jennie 'leaves' to Lutheran College in Los Angeles never to be seen again

1908   -Belle's farmhouse burns to the ground
-Four bodies are discovered in the ruins; three of Belle's children and one believed to be hers
-In May, Jennie Olson's body is found
-25 additional bodies are found on the farm

CELEBRATED CRIMINAL CASES OF AMERICA

BY

THOMAS S. DUKE
CAPTAIN OF POLICE. SAN FRANCISCO

PUBLISHED WITH APPROVAL OF THE HONORABLE BOARD OF
POLICE COMMISSIONERS OF SAN FRANCISCO

SAN FRANCISCO, CAL.
THE JAMES H. BARRY COMPANY
19 10

TWO YEARS AFTER BELLE WENT to the United States, she married a Swede named Albert Sorenson. They resided in Chicago and in 1900, Sorenson died under most suspicious circumstances. While it was said that he died from heart failure, his relatives were positive that he was poisoned, and as a motive for the deed, pointed to the fact that the widow collected the life insurance of $8,500 as soon as possible after his death. It is stated that an inquest was ordered, but for some reason the body was never exhumed.

Mrs. [Belle] Sorenson then moved to Austin, Ill., and a short time afterward her home was burned. A question arose as to the origin of the fire, but in the absence of proof of fraud the insurance companies were forced to pay the insurance.

She then returned to Chicago where she conducted a confectionery store at Grand avenue and Elizabeth street; which was subsequently gutted by fire. This mysterious fire resulted in another investigation by the insurance officials, but they were forced to pay her claim.

Shortly afterward she purchased a farm about six miles from La Porte, Indiana and married Peter Gunness a few months later.

In 1904, a meat chopper is said to have fallen off a shelf and split his head open, thus ending his existence. The weeping widow described to the coroner's jury how it fell from a shelf and struck her "poor husband's head," and in the absence of proof to the contrary, the statement was accepted as true.

At the time of the death of Gunness, [Belle] had three small children, named Philip, Myrtle and Lucy. She also had an adopted daughter named Jennie Olsen, who was fourteen years of age.

In September 1906, this girl disappeared, and Mrs. Gunness accounted for her absence by stating that she had sent her to Los Angeles to complete her education.

The woman then employed a man named Ray Lamphere to do the chores about the place. In 1906, she inserted an advertisement in the matrimonial columns of the leading papers of Chicago and other large cities, which read as follows:

"Personal—Comely widow who owns a large farm in one of the finest districts in La Porte County, Indiana, desires to make acquaintance of a gentleman equally well provided, with view of joining fortunes. No replies by letter considered unless sender is willing to follow answers with personal visit."

In May 1907, Ole B. Budsburg, a rather elderly widower residing in Iolo, Wisconsin, saw the advertisement, and as it looked good to him he decided to make a nice quiet investigation without telling his grown-up sons, Oscar and Mathew, a word about it.

The poor old gentleman left his home but never returned, and the last seen of him was when he negotiated the sale of a mortgage at the La Porte Savings Bank and drew the money on April 6, 1907.

In December 1907, Andrew Hegelein, a thrifty batchelor from Aberdeen, South Dakota, also corresponded with Mrs. Gunness. She replied that it would be advisable for him to come to the farm, and she suggested that he might sell out his business interests in South Dakota, as she was very favorably impressed with his letters.

As far as was convenient to do so, Hegelein, delighted with the headway he was making, complied with her request and repaired to her farm, arriving in January 1908. He had been at Mrs. Gunness' place about two weeks when he accompanied her to the Savings Bank in La Porte and presented a check for $2,900. But as he was unknown there and as the bankers would not accept the endorsement of Mrs. Gunness for this amount, they left the check there for collection. In a few days, the draft came, and the money was delivered to him, which she must have obtained. Almost immediately afterward she deposited $500 in that bank, $700 in the State Bank, and also paid numerous large bills.

A few days later Hegelein disappeared, and Mrs. Gunness stated that he had drawn the money for the purpose of going to Norway. He had a brother named A. K. Hegelein in Aberdeen, South Dakota, and as the weeks rolled by and he heard nothing from his brother, he became alarmed and wrote to Mrs. Gunness regarding his whereabouts.

In her reply she stated that all the information she could impart was the missing man's own statement to the effect that he drew his money with the intention of going to Norway. She expressed some apprehension over his failure to confide his plans to his brother, and she suggested in her letter that he sell out the remainder of his brother's stock along with his own and come to her farm, so that she might join him in an extensive search.

At 3:30 A.M. on April 28, 1908, Mrs. Gunness' home was burned to the ground. In the ruins, the charred remains of a woman and three children were found. The bodies of the little ones were at once identified as the remains of Mrs. Gunness' children, but as the woman's head was burned or cut off, there was some question as to whose remains they were.

Ray Lamphere, the farm hand, left her employ on February 3, 1908, because of a quarrel with Mrs. Gunness, and procured employment on a farm owned by John Wheatbrook, a short distance from the Gunness place.

After Lamphere left Mrs. Gunness, he frequently intimated that he could make it interesting for her if he wanted to talk, but her only response to this was that Lamphere was "crazy."

As it was proven conclusively that he was on the ground at the time the fire started, he was taken into custody by Sheriff Smulzer.

The mysterious remarks made by Lamphere in regard to making trouble for Mrs. Gunness were recalled, and a most thorough investigation was instituted, with the result that five more mutilated and decomposed bodies were found buried in the backyard on May 5.

One was identified as the body of Jennie Olsen Gunness, the sixteen-year-old adopted daughter of Mrs. Gunness, who was supposed to be in Los Angeles completing her education. It is presumed that she was murdered because she knew too much regarding the death of Peter Gunness in 1904.

The second body was that of Andrew Hegelein from South Dakota. The third was the unidentified body of a man, and the fourth and fifth were the bodies of two eight-year-old girls. On May 6, four additional bodies of men were unearthed in the backyard.

In most instances the limbs were removed from the bodies in such a manner as to indicate that the amputations were performed by someone familiar with anatomy. The theory is that some of the bodies were too heavy for the woman to handle as a whole.

On May 9, two more bundles of bones, decayed flesh and clothing were found in the private graveyard, but the ravages of decomposition made identification impossible. On May 14, a few bones of one more victim were found in the ashes in the cellar.

In view of these discoveries, a serious doubt arose as to the actual fate of Mrs. Gunness. It was suspected that in addition to murdering her children and several others, she had unveiled some unsuspecting woman into her home, and after killing her, disfigured her remains in such a manner that they could not be recognized, and after setting fire to the house, escaped; believing it would be taken for granted that the charred remains of the woman were those of herself and that no further search would be made for her. This theory proved incorrect, for on May 16 a lower jawbone was found in the ashes and was taken to Dr. Morton, a dentist in La Porte for examination. Some dentistry work was plainly visible on the teeth which still adhered to the jawbone which he positively identified as work done for Mrs. Gunness a year previously. Rings found on the fingers of the dead woman were also identified as the property of Mrs. Gunness.

There was a difference of opinion as to how Mrs. Gunness met her death. The theory of the prosecution was that she was burned to death, but Dr. J. Meyers gave it as his opinion that death was caused by contraction of the heart, probably due to strychnine poisoning, which was the poison used in killing Hegelein and several other victims.

Shortly after Mrs. Gunness' private graveyard was discovered, Oscar and Mathew Budsburg came to La Porte, as they suspected that their aged father, who had mysteriously disappeared from his home in Lolo. Wis., in May 1907, might have fallen into this woman's trap. Their suspicions proved to be well founded, for they identified one of the bodies as that of their missing father.

Olof Lindboe of Chicago stated that his brother, Thomas, had worked for Mrs. Gunness three years previously, and the last letter he had received from him contained the information that Thomas intended to marry his employer. As Olof heard nothing more from his brother, he wrote to Mrs. Gunness, who replied that Thomas had gone to St. Louis, but Olof never heard from him again.

On May 12, the surgical instruments with which the bodies were probably dismembered, were found in the ashes.

On May 19, Miss Jennie Graham of Waukesha, Wis., arrived in La Porte to inquire regarding her brother, who had left home to marry a rich widow in La Porte, but who was never heard from after that. As most of the bodies were badly mutilated and decomposed, it was impossible to ascertain if her brother's remains were among them.

Henry Gurholdt of Scandinavia, Wis., corresponded with Mrs. Gunness, and then took $1,500 with him to La Porte and was never seen again, but a watch found with one of the bodies was exactly the same in appearance as the one he wore.

Mrs. Marie Svenherud of Christiania, Norway, made inquiry through Acting Consul Faye of Chicago for her son Olof, who had written her that he was about to leave Chicago for La Porte to marry a rich Norwegian widow. He had become acquainted through the agency of the matrimonial advertisement column of a newspaper. The mother added that she never heard from her son again.

After the disappearance of Hegelein, Lamphere was seen wearing an overcoat which belonged to the former, and on May 18 a watch which was in the possession of Lamphere at the time of his arrest was identified by J. G. Ramden of Manfred, N. D,, as the property of his half brother, John Moe of Elbow Lake, Minn., who left his home in 1907, ostensibly to marry a widow in La Porte, but was never heard from afterward. Lamphere stated that Mrs. Gunness had presented him with the watch.

When first interrogated as to his whereabouts on the night of the fire, Lamphere claimed that he was in the company of a negress named Mrs. Elizabeth Smith until 4 A.M., or one-half hour after the fire started, but he subsequently confessed that he burned the Gunness home but denied that he had committed murder.

Lamphere and a neighbor named Fred Brickman stated that they dug trenches for Mrs. Gunness at different times, but that they had no knowledge as to for what purpose they were used.

On May 22, 1908, Lamphere was indicted for the murder of the Gunness family by means of arson, and also on the charge of accessory in the murder of Hegelein. He pleaded guilty of arson and was sentenced to imprisonment for an indeterminate period of from two to twenty years. Immediately after his conviction Lamphere's health failed rapidly, and he died on December 30, 1909. On January 14, 1910, Rev. E. A. Schell made public a confession made by Lamphere shortly after his arrest, in which he admitted that he helped Mrs. Gunness to bury one of the victims and saw her chloroform another after felling him with a hatchet. He also confessed that he chloroformed the Gunness family, but claimed that Mrs. Smith, a negress with whom he had spent a portion of the night, assisted him, and that it was she who set the house on fire.

As there was no evidence to substantiate the charge against the negress, she was never prosecuted. It is the opinion of Attorney Ralph Smith that the negress did not accompany Lamphere on this night.

H. H. Holmes
(May 16, 1861 – May 7, 1896)

HE WAS AN AMERIAN SERIAL KILLER who was active between 1891 and 1894. He confessed to murdering 27 people, often in his "murder castle" which consisted of a maze-like structure to trap his victims. However, investigators could confirm only nine murders. Later, he had said he killed as many as 200 people, but his claim couldn't be proven (it was most likely exaggerated).

H. H. Holmes was born in Gilmanton, New Hampshire to Levi Horton Mudgett and Theodate Page Price. Holmes had a disciplinarian father and was bullied as a child. He later graduated from the University of Michigan Medical School in the year 1884. However, while enrolled, he stole bodies and disfigured the corpses. Soon after graduating, he moved to Chicago and practiced pharmacy. In addition to this, he began cutting real estate, business, and promotional deals using his alias H. H. Holmes. He married Clara A. Lovering in 1878. He stayed with her for until he strayed away, and Clara ended up moving to New Hampshire.

Holmes later went to Minneapolis, Minnesota and met Myrta Z. Belknap. Though still married to Clara, he married Myrta Z. Belknap in 1887 under the alias Henry Howard Holmes. He tried to file for a divorce from Clara but it was never finalized. Two years later, the two has a daughter named Lucy. Holmes lived with Myrta and Lucy in Wilmette, Illinois but spent much of his time in Chicago for business. Holmes eventually strayed away from his wife and daughter.

Holmes later married Georgiana Yoke in 1894 in Denver, Colorado while still being married to Clara and Myrta. In addition, he had a relationship with Julia Smythe, a married woman, later Holmes' first victim.

Holmes bought a drugstore from Dr. E.S. Holton, the drugstore owner's wife, Mrs. Holton while Dr. Holton was dying of cancer. When Holton died, Holmes took over the store and killed Mrs. Holton and had the store to himself. Holmes built his notorious three-story hotel called World's Fair Hotel, known as the "Murder Castle" by law enforcement officers and later nationwide, which he opened as a hotel in 1893. He built stairways that lead to nowhere, doorways that opened to brick walls, soundproof rooms, and other maze-like structures to trap his victims in the hotel. His victims were mostly women who would stay at the hotel during the nearby 1893 World Fair, a few men and children, and many employees who he made take out insurance policies with him as the beneficiary.

Holmes had a wide variety of methodology. He often locked his victims in a soundproof vault and murdered them. He brutally murdered many of his victims, but many also died via gas chamber, poison, and several other methods. Many of the boys we dismembered, burned, and put some in quicklime vats so they would quickly decompose. Some bodies he sold for scientific research.

Holmes was finally apprehended for the murder of his business partner, Benjamin Pitezel and Pitezel's family. Holmes and Pitezel planned to fake Pitezel's own death so his wife could claim insurance money and Holmes would get a portion of it. However, Holmes ended up murdering Pitezel and convinced his wife to give him all the money. Holmes manipulated Pitezel's wife to let three of her five children stay in his custody. Holmes traveled with the children north into Canada. He killed two of Pitezel's daughters in Toronto and his son in Philadelphia. The boy's teeth and bits of bones were later found. The police did an investigation and discovered the Benjamin Pitezel and three of his children, among many others, and the secrets of the murder.

Holmes was hung at the Philadelphia County prison on May 7, 1896. Holmes died slowly as it took him 15 to 20 minutes to die; his neck didn't immediately snap. Holmes requested his grave be filled with concrete so his body could not be dug up. His request was granted. However, in 2017 his body was exhumed and taken for testing after suspicion arose that Holmes escaped his death. The body was identified as Holmes' and he was reburied.

TIMELINE

1861   -On May 16, Herman Webster Mudgett is born

1884   -Holmes works in an anatomy lab

1886   -Holmes kills a classmate named Dr. Robert Lee for insurance money

1887   -Construction begins on a mixed use building known as the Murder Castle

1891   -His mistress Julia Smythe and her daughter Pearl "disappear" in December

1892   -Holmes becomes friends with Benjamin Pitezel; his right hand man for fraud schemes

1894   -Holmes is arrested in Missouri for selling mortgaged goods
- He makes bail in July
-In July, Pitezel fakes his death so his wife can collect a life insurance policy
-Holmes kills Benjamin Pitezel
-On November 17, Holmes is arrested on an outstanding warrant for horse theft in Texas
-Alice and Nellie Pitezel are murdered

1895   -On July 15, Alice and Nellie, bodies are found in a
        cellar in Toronto
        -The bones and teeth of Howard Pitezel are found
        -In October, Holmes is put on trial for the murder of
        Benjamin Pitezel and the Pitezel children
        -He confesses to murdering at least 27 people in
        Chicago, Indianapolis, and Toronto
        -The Murder Castle was set on fire and gutted in August

1896   -On May 7th, Holmes is sentenced to the death penalty
        and is hung

2017   -Holmes' body is exhumed for testing after allegations
        arose that Holmes escaped death;
        -The body is Holmes' and he is reburied

CELEBRATED CRIMINAL CASES OF AMERICA

BY

THOMAS S. DUKE
CAPTAIN OF POLICE. SAN FRANCISCO

PUBLISHED WITH APPROVAL OF THE HONORABLE BOARD OF
POLICE COMMISSIONERS OF SAN FRANCISCO

SAN FRANCISCO, CAL.
THE JAMES H. BARRY COMPANY
19 10

108

HISTORY OF THE CRIMINAL OF THE CENTURY, HERMAN W. MUDGETT, ALIAS H. H. HOLMES, WHO MURDERED NUMEROUS PEOPLE, INCLUDING WOMEN AND CHILDREN.
(From Detective Frank Geyer's History.)

HERMAN W. MUDGETT WAS born in Gilmanton, NH. on May 16, 1860, but spent his boyhood days on a farm near Burlington, VT.

He was extremely bright, ambitious and studious, and at the age of sixteen years he became a schoolteacher.

On July 4, 1878, at the age of eighteen, he married Clara A. Lovering at Alton, NH., and about this time he gave up his position as a schoolteacher to enable him to take a course in a medical school at Burlington, VT.

A year later he finished his course at this school and then went to Ann Arbor College, Michigan, to complete his education.

In 1881, Mudgett gained possession of a body that bore a remarkable resemblance to a fellow student who was his closest friend and who had taken out a life insurance policy for $1,000 a short time previously, in which Mudgett was named as beneficiary.

This put an idea into the heads of the two students. They surreptitiously placed this body in the bed of Mudgett's friend, who immediately disappeared.

There was evidently little, or no investigation made regarding the case, as Mudgett collected the insurance without trouble, and presumably divided it with his "dead" chum. Shortly after this Mudgett left college, and under the name of Holmes procured a position at an insane asylum in Norristown, PA.

After six months he left this position and proceeded to Philadelphia, where he procured employment as a drug clerk.

He next went to Chicago, where he opened a drug store of his own. Continuing to use the name Holmes, he married Miss Myrta Belknap in Chicago, on January 28, 1887, thus committing bigamy.

On January 17, 1894, under the name of Howard, he again

married in Denver, Miss Georgie Yoke, of St. Louis, she soon became his first victim.

Before marrying Miss Yoke, Holmes traveled about the country under numerous assumed names, engaging in various enterprises, none of which would bear investigation. He accumulated considerable money and constructed a four-story building at the corner of 63 and Wallace Street in Chicago, which was known as "Holmes Castle."

About 1889, Holmes met Benjamin F. Pitezel in Chicago, who was afterward suspected of being Holmes' partner in many crimes.

At that time Pitezel's family, consisting of a wife and four small children, named Dessie, Alice, Nellie and Howard, lived in St. Louis.

Holmes was a man of medium height and build. He was immaculate in appearance, suave[1] in manners and as this narrative will show, fiendish in disposition.

Pitezel was a mesmeric subject, and Holmes, being possessed of hypnotic powers, discovered this fact, and thereafter Pitezel was so much clay in his hands.

On November 9, 1893, Pitezel took out a $10,000 life insurance policy from the Fidelity Mutual Life Association of Philadelphia, which was made payable to his wife.

Holmes, knowing this, suggested to Pitezel and his wife that Pitezel go to Philadelphia, and under the assumed name of B. F. Perry, open up an office and put up a sign "Patents Bought and Sold."

Holmes stated that he would then institute a search among hospitals or medical colleges and find a body having features and physique similar to Pitezel. The body would be surreptitiously placed in the establishment and laid in such a position as to so clearly indicate that death had resulted from an accidental explosion that no questions would be asked. Pitezel would disappear and Mrs. Pitezel's fourteen-year-old daughter, Alice, would journey to Philadelphia and identify the remains as those of her father. The insurance money would be paid without question, and then Pitezel would quietly return to his family. Mrs. Pitezel offered strenuous objections to the plan, but Holmes commanded

1. Charming, confident

Pitezel to do his bidding, and the result was that on August 17, 1894, Pitezel opened his office at 1316 Callowhill Street and put out his sign as directed.

On June 15, 1894, while Holmes, then known as Howard, was in St. Louis arranging details for his latest scheme, he purchased a drug store, upon which he gave a mortgage. Shortly afterward he sold this mortgaged property, and on July 19 he was arrested on a charge of obtaining money by false pretenses in connection with this sale.

While in jail he met Marion Hedgepeth, who, with three others, robbed a train near St. Louis in 1891, and was captured in San Francisco. Holmes asked Hedgepeth if he knew of any slick lawyer. The train robber recommended him to J. D. Howe, of St. Louis, and Holmes then foolishly unfolded his whole scheme in regard to Pitezel, to Hedgepeth, and told him that he would give him $500 for his services if the plan worked. On July 31, Holmes was released on bail furnished by his third "wife." A few days after being released he proceeded to Philadelphia, where he met Pitezel, alias Perry, and on August 17, the day on which the latter opened his office in Callowhill Street, Holmes accompanied him to a secondhand furniture store located at 1037 Buttonwood Street and assisted him in selecting furniture.

On August 22, a carpenter named Eugene Smith, who was of an inventive turn of mind, passed this office, and being attracted by the sign, stepped in to discuss the merits of a set-saw he had invented and desired to put on the market. "Perry" listened attentively to his description of the invention and asked him to bring a model the next day. Smith complied with the request, and after an examination of it, Perry predicted heavy sales.

On Monday, September 3, Smith called to ascertain how his device was selling. "Perry" was not in the office, but his hat and coat were there, and Smith, believing he had stepped out for a few moments, waited until he became impatient and left. He returned the next day and again saw no one but observed that the coat and hat were in the same position. He then made inquiry in the neighborhood and learned that "Perry" had not been seen since Saturday.

His suspicions being aroused he decided to investigate. As "Perry" occupied both floors of the small two-story building, Smith proceeded upstairs, and in a back room he found the mutilated body of Perry. The breast and side of the face were badly burned; fragments of a large bottle were found near the corpse, and a tobacco pipe and a burned match were also found.

The body was removed to the morgue, and after lying there until September 13 without being claimed, it was buried in the potter's field.

On September 19, Attorney Howe called on Mrs. Pitezel in St. Louis and informed her that her husband was dead and requested that the fourteen-year-old daughter, Alice, accompany him to Philadelphia for the purpose of identifying the remains. Mrs. Pitezel then signed a paper prepared by Howe, which gave him power of attorney to collect the money, and he left with Alice, Mrs. Pitezel believing that the child would be instructed to identify the body of a stranger and that her husband was alive and well.

On September 21, Howe, Alice, Holmes and Smith, who discovered the body, called at the Philadelphia office of the insurance company, and after Smith was interrogated, the party proceeded with the insurance officials to disinter the remains. Holmes explained that he was a close friend of the Pitezel family and knew that Pitezel was located at 1316 Callowhill Street, under the assumed name of Perry, because of financial troubles in Fort Worth.

When the body was exposed, Alice Pitezel and Holmes immediately identified the remains as those of Pitezel. While the cause of Pitezel's death was not perfectly clear to the insurance officials, they concluded that the large bottle which was found broken by his side contained some inflammable substance which exploded as the victim was evidently in the act of lighting his pipe.

Against this theory it was argued that the body reclined in a peaceful attitude and the stomach when opened gave forth a distinct odor of chloroform.

At any rate, the insurance money was paid to Howe, who proceeded to St. Louis and paid Mrs. Pitezel the $10,000, less $2,800 deducted for expenses. As Alice did not accompany Howe, Mrs. Pitezel anxiously inquired as to her whereabouts, but the attorney assured her that Holmes would see that she was well provided for. A few days after this, Holmes visited Mrs. Pitezel who begged piteously to be taken forthwith to her husband and child.

Holmes told her that she must be patient, as the insurance officials were suspicious of the entire transaction and that he considered it advisable for the family to remain separated for the present; in fact, he stated that he had come to get the two smaller children, Nellie and Howard, and take them to Covington, KY., where a nice old lady was caring for Alice.

Mrs. Pitezel made strenuous objections to this plan, but after some argument, Holmes persuaded her to consent to their going.

The monster then produced a note on which he stated that he and Mr. Pitezel had obtained $16,000 from Attorney Samuels in Fort Worth, and in order to save their property there a portion of the amount must be forwarded immediately.

In this manner he obtained $7,000 from her, and after instructing her to proceed to the home of her parents in Galva, Ill., he departed on September 28 with the two children, after promising that the entire family would be reunited at the earliest possible moment.

At this time Alice was in the keeping of a lady in Covington, KY., and at Holmes' request she wrote a cheerful letter to her mother in which she spoke of the kind treatment accorded to her. This greatly increased Mrs. Pitezel's confidence in Holmes, and she ceased to regret parting with the other two children.

Immediately after the letter was forwarded, Holmes had Alice meet him and the other two children in Indianapolis, and from thence they journeyed to Cincinnati.

He left Cincinnati on October 1 with the three children and proceeded to Indianapolis, where he put the children in the Circle Hotel and then met Miss Yoke and stopped with her at another hotel in the neighborhood. This lady believed herself to be Holmes' lawful wife and knew nothing of his misdeeds.

He represented that he was endeavoring to place a patent copier on the market with which he expected to make a fortune, and that his mysterious journeys were in connection with this business. He planned so that Miss Yoke never met the children.

The next day Holmes took Alice and Nellie to Detroit, but little Howard had mysteriously disappeared. Holmes wrote for Mrs. Pitezel to bring the baby and Dessie to Detroit, where they were to meet Mr. Pitezel. Holmes and his "wife" stopped at one hotel, the two girls at another, and when Mrs. Pitezel arrived, she stopped at Geis's Hotel, a very short distance from the New Western, where Alice and Nellie were staying, under the name of Canning, that being the name of their grandparents.

Holmes instructed the children to remain in their room, and when he met Mrs. Pitezel, he stated that an investigation had been instituted and he deemed it necessary to delay the reunion of the family. As to the investigation, Holmes unconsciously spoke the truth.

It will be recalled that he promised to pay Marion Hedgepeth $500 if the insurance swindle was consummated, but as time rolled by and Marion saw nothing of the money, he decided to turn informer for two reasons: First, to get revenge, and second, to gain the good will of those who might be able to assist him. So on October 9, he wrote a letter to Chief of Police Harrigan of St. Louis, wherein he exposed the entire scheme, but of course he did not believe that Pitezel was dead.

On October 18, Holmes took his "wife," Nellie, and Alice Pitezel to Toronto, Canada, he and his wife stopping at the Walker House under the name of Howell, and the children were registered at the Albion under the name of Canning, as in Detroit.

Mrs. Pitezel was instructed by Holmes to leave on October 19 for Toronto, with Dessie and the baby, and if he deemed it safe, she could there join the remainder of the family. By this time the poor woman was almost insane from grief, as she began to fear the worst. She asked Holmes to allow her husband to write to her, but he stated that the authorities might intercept the letters.

Holmes called on Mrs. Pitezel in Toronto and told her it was impossible to reunite the family at that time, and he sent her with Dessie and the baby, Wharton, to Ogdensburg, N.Y., and thence to Burlington, VT., where Holmes rented a house at 26 Winooski

Avenue, where he intended to murder the remainder of the family, but fortunately the opportunity did not present itself. (After the family left this house, a large bottle of chloroform was found in the cellar where it had been left by Holmes.)

The mother now began to lose hope of ever seeing her husband and three children again, and she finally returned to her relatives in Galva, Ill.

Pleading urgent business, Holmes left Miss Yoke about November 1 and went to Gilmanton, where he remained with his legal wife until November 17, when he went to Boston. The detectives got on his trail while he was at his old home and traced him to Boston, where he was arrested on November 19. His effects were searched, and several letters were found which had been written by the Pitezel children to their mother.

Holmes believed that the authorities either suspected him of having substituted a body, falsely claiming it was Pitezel's, or wanted him for horse stealing in Texas.

Having in mind the manner in which horse thieves were frequently punished in Texas he immediately stated that he had defrauded the insurance company by swearing the body found on Callowhill Street was Pitezel's, when, as a matter of fact, he stated, Pitezel had left America with his three children.

He expressed a willingness to return to Philadelphia and plead guilty to the insurance swindle charge, providing he was not turned over to the Texas authorities. As he made a statement in which he claimed Mrs. Pitezel was a party to the fraud, she was arrested and brought to Boston with Dessie and the baby. Mrs. Pitezel was subjected to a severe cross-examination, but at it concluded, the authorities were convinced that she was innocent. However, on November 19, Mrs. Pitezel and Holmes were taken to Philadelphia as prisoners, the two children and Miss Yoke accompanying the party. It was June 3, 1895, before Holmes was brought to trial for defrauding the insurance company. He willingly pleaded guilty.

At this time several months had elapsed since either Pitezel or his three children had been heard from, and the authorities were becoming convinced that Holmes was guilty of far worse crimes than defrauding an insurance company by substituting a body. They strongly suspected that he was guilty of at least four murders.

As Pitezel was suspected of having an intimate knowledge of Holmes' criminal career, it can be seen that his desire to permanently seal Pitezel's lips was only equaled by his desire to obtain the bulk of his life insurance. Mrs. Pitezel would eventually realize this, and if her husband was not returned to her, she would inform the authorities, with the result that the body in the potter's field would be subjected to a closer examination, which would mean that Holmes would probably be charged with the murder of Pitezel.

The older children were probably informed by their mother of the insurance swindle and were assured that their father would return, and of course children talk. The officers assumed that Holmes realized all this and that he decided that his safety was assured only after the entire family was disposed of. He could not hope to kill six people at once without being detected, so he decided to separate them and murder them one by one.

On December 27, 1894, Holmes made another statement substantially as follows:

"I regret that I have made false statements in the past, but the following are the facts: "While Pitezel was at 1316 Callowhill Street, he drank very heavily and I took him to task about it. He appeared to be despondent and said that he had better drink enough to kill himself and have done with it all. The next morning, I visited his place and using a key I entered the building. I found a letter addressed to me, which I destroyed, in which he said I would find his body upstairs. I went upstairs and found him lying dead on the floor. There was a rubber tube in his mouth which was attached to a quill run through a cork in a large bottle containing chloroform.

"I had arranged with Pitezel that the body substituted for his should be burned about the face and hands by pouring a mixture of benzene, chloroform, and ammonia on it and then setting it on fire; that a large bottle was then to be broken and a smoking pipe and burned match placed nearby; the object being to show that the person supposed to be Pitezel or Perry, had actually ignited the mixture in the bottle while lighting the pipe, and that the bottle exploded and death was caused by the burns. Seeing Pitezel's body, I decided to carry out this plan in all its details. The three children are now in Europe in the custody of Miss Minnie Williams, formerly of Fort Worth, Texas."

It was easily proved that Holmes told the truth regarding the identity of the dead man found in Callowhill Street, but the remainder of the statement was not believed.

It was now clear that Holmes was not guilty of substituting a body, and action regarding that case was postponed, pending a further search for the missing children.

The District Attorney then looked about for a detective possessed of sufficient ability and determination to undertake this gigantic task, and he decided upon Frank Geyer, of the Philadelphia Police Department.

As eight months had elapsed since the children were last seen, and as it was probable that persons who had seen them had forgotten their faces, it can be readily understood that the obstacles confronting this officer were apparently insurmountable.

On June 26, 1895, he started out with photographs of Holmes and the three children.

He proceeded to Cincinnati and began visiting the hotels. When he reached the Hotel Bristol at Sixth and Vine Street, the clerk identified the pictures as those of a man and three children who registered under the name of Cook.

It was the detective's theory that Holmes had murdered the children in some house in the suburbs of some city, so he began to make rounds of the real estate offices, both in the city and in the suburbs. When he arrived at the office of J. C. Thomas, at 15 East Third Street, the clerk recognized the picture of Holmes and Howard Pitezel, and it was learned that Holmes had rented a house at 305 Poplar Street, where he only remained two days. Geyer proceeded there and interviewed a Miss Hill who resided next door.

She saw Holmes moving an immense stove into the house, but no furniture.

The singular incident so impressed her that she unconsciously watched the proceeding very closely. Holmes observed this and decided to change his plans, but before leaving the house with Howard he offered the stove to the "inquisitive" lady.

Geyer then proceeded to Indianapolis and visited the hotels and real estate offices. He gathered valuable information as to the route taken by the children from the letters which they wrote to their mother, but which Holmes withheld and foolishly kept in his possession.

Here Mr. Herman Ackelow was located, and he at once identified the pictures of the children as those of guests who stopped with him when he conducted the Circle House. He also stated that the children were held in their room practically as prisoners, and although they were constantly crying, they refused to state the cause of their grief. In a letter written by Alice to her mother just after they left Indianapolis, and which was found in Holmes' pocket when arrested, the girl innocently remarked that "Howard" (meaning her brother) "is not with us now."

This convinced Geyer that the child had been murdered in or near Indianapolis, but he failed to obtain any clue at that time upon which to work.

The detective then proceeded to "Holmes Castle" in Chicago, but he learned nothing there regarding the Pitezel children. He then proceeded to Detroit and found that on October 12, Nellie and Alice Pitezel were registered at the New Western Hotel, but neither Howard nor the trunk were seen there.

Thinking that Holmes might have had Howard and the trunk with him, Geyer proceeded to learn where Holmes stopped, and found that he and Miss Yoke were registered as "G. Howell and wife" at the Normandie, but as neither the boy nor the trunk were seen at this place, the detective became more convinced than ever as to where little Howard met his fate. But intent on tracing the girls first, Geyer proceeded to Toronto, Canada, where Mrs. Pitezel next met Holmes.

He arrived on Monday, July 8, and found that Holmes and Miss Yoke registered on October 18, 1894, at the Walker House, under the name of Howell and wife, and that the children were registered at the Albion Hotel under the name of Canning. Herbert Jones, the chief clerk of this hotel, stated that on October 25, Holmes called for the children, paid their bill, and they were never seen again.

As it was known that Holmes went to his first wife in Gilmanton a few days after this, Geyer became convinced that the fiend had rented a house in Toronto for the purpose of murdering the two girls.

He prepared a list of all real estate agents and had the newspapers publish the pictures of the children and print his theories.

He then began a canvas of the real estate offices, which lasted for days, but nothing was accomplished. Finally, Greyer learned that a Mrs. Frank Nudel had rented a house at No. 16 Vincent Street, in October 1894, to a man who only remained there a few days and acted quite mysteriously. He immediately proceeded to the house, but when he reached the house located at No. 18 Vincent Street, he showed the pictures of Holmes and Alice to Mr. Thomas Ryves, who resided there, and that gentleman instantly recognized them as the photographs of a man and girl who were at the house next door for a day and then disappeared.

Mr. Ryves furthermore stated that this man borrowed a spade from him, saying he wanted to plant some potatoes.

On receiving this information, Geyer hurried to the home of Mrs. Nudel, and when he showed the lady and her daughter Holmes' picture and asked them if they had ever seen the man, they instantly replied that it was the picture of the man who rented their Vincent Street property. Geyer's enthusiasm now knew no bounds. He rushed back to No. 18 Vincent Street and borrowing the same shovel Holmes had used, proceeded to the next house. No. 16, where a family named Armbrust was then living.

After hurriedly making known his mission, the lady told him to proceed with his investigation.

He examined the house, and on raising the linoleum in the kitchen he discovered a trap door which led to a dark cellar.

He procured a light, and after examining the ground he found a spot which appeared to have been recently disturbed. He had only been digging a minute or two when a terrible odor arose which became more horrible with each shovelful of dirt removed. He finally unearthed what was apparently the arm of a child, but as the flesh fell from the bones, he decided that great caution would be necessary, or the bodies would fall to pieces. So, Undertaker Humphreys was called in and the digging proceeded, with the result that the terribly decomposed bodies of Nellie and Alice Pitezel were found.

While the features of the children could not be recognized, the clothing and hair were readily identified by the heartbroken mother, who started for Toronto as soon as she was advised of the discovery. To make "assurance doubly sure," Geyer located a family named McDonald, who moved into the house after Holmes left, and they found a wooden egg, from which, when parted in the middle, a little "snake" would spring out, Mrs. Pitezel recognized this as a toy she had purchased for her little girls.

These bodies were entirely nude when found, and the clothing spoken of above was taken from the dead children by Holmes and stuffed up in the chimney in the parlor with some straw and set on fire, but as they did not burn, the chimney was left in a clogged condition, and Mrs. Armbrust on examining it found the clothes and fortunately did not dispose of them.

It is perhaps needless to say that Holmes' object in removing and destroying the clothes was to prevent the bodies from being identified.

On July 19, after the burial of the Pitezel children in Toronto, Geyer proceeded to Detroit, where he learned that Holmes had rented a house at 241 East Forest Avenue, and an investigation showed that he had dug a grave in the cellar, but before he had an opportunity to complete his work, information reached him that detectives were on his trail, and he abandoned his plans for the time being.

Geyer left Detroit on July 23 and returned to Indianapolis to search for little Howard Pitezel's body. For days and days, he made a tireless round of the real estate offices both in the city and for miles out into the suburbs.

On August 1, he went to Chicago as a child's skeleton had been found at "Holmes Castle," but Geyer became convinced that this was the remains of some other unfortunate child, and in a few days he returned to Indianapolis. The search now included all the small towns within a radius of several miles from the city.

After nearly a month's work, no place remained unsearched but the pretty little town of Irvington, about six miles from Indianapolis. In this town Mr. Geyer, who was now almost exhausted, wearily made his way to the real estate office of an elderly man named Brown. After relating his story and showing his pictures hundreds of times, after weeks of fruitless labor and nights of restless sleep, Geyer again related his story and showed his pictures of Holmes.

The old man adjusted his glasses and finally remarked that it was the picture of a man who rented a house from him in October 1894.

As the house belonged to a Dr. Thompson, who had seen the tenant, Geyer, who had now taken a new lease of life, hurried to him, and the doctor not only identified the picture as a likeness of his tenant, but told the detective that a boy in his employ named Elvet Moorman had seen this man with a boy at the house.

When interviewed, Elvet immediately identified the pictures of Holmes and little Howard.

He stated that his duty compelled him to go and milk a cow every afternoon, which was kept in a lot in the rear of the house Holmes rented, and that while so engaged, Holmes asked him to help him put up a stove when he had finished milking.

The boy complied with the request and while assisting Holmes, he asked him why he did not use a gas stove instead of a coal stove, and Holmes replied that "gas was not healthy for children." Little Howard was present when this remark was made.

Geyer then proceeded to the vacant cottage which was across the street from a Methodist church. He searched the house from cellar to roof and discovered nothing. He then looked through the lattice[2] work between the piaza floor and the ground and saw some pieces of an old trunk.

He broke in after this and found that in one place on the remains of the trunk, a piece of blue calico had been pasted, and on this calico was the figure of a flower. As the earth appeared to have been disturbed, Geyer began digging with a vengeance, but all in vain.

2. Wood or metal used as a screen, fence, or support

He then proceeded to the barn, and there found an immense coal stove. As it was growing late, Geyer quit for the night with the intention of resuming the search in the morning.

Mrs. Pitezel was then with her folks in Galva, Ill, and Geyer telegraphed this query: "Did the missing trunk have blue calico with white flowers over seam on bottom?" and the answer was, "Yes."

When Geyer left the cottage, two boys named Walter Jenny and Oscar Kettenbach, who knew of Geyer's mission, decided to "play detective." They began looking for evidence in the cottage and ran their busy hands into a stovepipe hole in the chimney in the basement. They brought out a handful of ashes, but in those ashes were several teeth and small pieces of bone. While Geyer was still in the telegraph office at Irvington, he was informed of this discovery and rushed back to the cottage.

Procuring a hammer and chisel he tore down the lower part of the chimney and found almost a full set of children's teeth, several pieces of human bone, and a large charred mass which proved to be a portion of a child's stomach, liver and spleen, baked hard.

The corner grocer then came forward and announced that the boy, whose picture Geyer showed him, came to his store in October and left his coat there, saying that he would call for it, but never returned.

Mrs. Pitezel was again sent for and she identified the coat as one belonging to little Howard.

Geyer then located Albert Schiffling, who conducted a shop at 48 Virginia Avenue, Indianapolis, and he stated that on October 3, Holmes, accompanied by little Howard, called on him and left some surgical instruments to be sharpened. But the child little realized that they were being sharpened for the purpose of dismembering his body so that it could be cremated in the stove afterward set up.

A coroner's jury, after hearing the evidence, had no hesitancy in rendering a verdict to the effect that Howard Pitezel was murdered by Holmes.

On September 1, 1895, Detective Geyer returned to Philadelphia, and after being congratulated on all sides for unraveling one of the greatest mysteries in criminal history in America, he proceeded to bring the archfiend to justice.

Holmes having been indicted for the murder of Benjamin Pitezel, the trial was set for October 28. While Detective Geyer was engaged in locating missing members of the Pitezel family, the authorities in Chicago, Fort Worth, Texas, and numerous other cities were investigating Holmes' career previous to the death of Pitezel's.

When the officials inspected "Holmes Castle" at Sixty-third and Wallace Street in Chicago, they were astounded at the elaborate preparations made by this criminal to trap his victims and dispose of their remains right in the heart of a great city.

This structure was a four-story brick building covering a lot about 50x120 feet. The lower floor was occupied by stores, a drug store being on the corner; the outside rooms of the three upper stories having square bay windows and were arranged into apartments and offices, with the exception of that part used by Holmes in connection with his human slaughter-house. His rooms were on the second floor, and in his office was a vault from which neither air nor could sound escape when the door was closed.

From his bathroom, which had no windows and no means of lighting, unless an artificial light was brought in, was a secret stairway leading to the basement, and in order to reach this stairway the rug in the bathroom was raised, and there was found a trap door. The laboratory on the third floor was connected with the cellar in a similar manner. There was no other means of reaching this particular part of the cellar except by these secret stairs.

In this cellar was a large grate with a removable iron covering in front, and under this grate was a large firebox. In an ash pile in the corner several small pieces of burned human bone were found, and in the center of the room was a long dissecting table, upon which was found blood and in- dentures from surgical instruments.

On July 24, 1895, Detectives Fitzpatrick and Norton, of the Chicago police, began a systematic search for evidence of crime committed by Holmes in this building. They dug up the cellar, and buried in quicklime they found seventeen ribs, three sections of vertebrae of the spinal column, and several teeth attached to the upper portion of a jaw bone. A part of a child's cape coat, which was decayed and lime-eaten, and a woman's garment thoroughly saturated with blood and brown with age were also found. These discoveries were all taken to Dr. C. P. Stingfield, and after a microscopical examination, he declared that the stains on the woman's garment were human blood and that the bones were portions of the anatomy of children from eight to fourteen years of age. In one of his numerous statements, Holmes claimed that the Pitezel children had gone to Europe in care of a Miss Minnie Williams. This resulted in an investigation as to the identity of Miss Williams and also resulted in two more murders being charged to Holmes.

Miss Williams entered Holmes' employ as a stenographer in 1893. At this time, he was at the head of the so-called "Campbell Yates Manufacturing Company," with "offices" in the castle.

Learning that she and her sister, Annie owned a valuable piece of land in Fort Worth, Texas, he professed love to Miss Minnie, and it is said that they lived as man and wife in the castle. In the later part of 1893 Minnie, at Holmes' request, wrote to Annie that she was about to be married, and requested Annie, who was a teacher in an academy at Fort Worth, to proceed to Chicago at once to attend the wedding.

Annie arrived in Chicago shortly afterward, but within a short time both girls mysteriously disappeared and were never seen again.

In February 1894, Pitezel, under the name of Lyman, proceeded to Fort Worth from Chicago and placed a deed on record from one Bond to Lyman for a valuable piece of ground at Second and Rusk Street.

"Bond" was supposed to have been obtained by the title from Minnie Williams. On this property, "Lyman" began erecting a building, and shortly afterward, Holmes alias "Pratt," appeared on the scene.

Their business affairs became badly muddled, and they left town before the building was completed, but not before Holmes stole a horse and engaged in numerous other shady transactions.

On July 19, 1895, the police made another search of the castle and found more charred bones, several metal buttons, and part of a watch chain. C. E. Davis, who formerly conducted a jewelry store in the castle, identified the watch chain as belonging to Minnie Williams, and also stated that he repaired it on two occasions. He furthermore stated that he had seen Minnie Williams wearing a dress on which were buttons similar to those found.

On August 4, Detective Fitzpatrick found Minnie Williams' trunk in janitor Pat. Quinlan's room in the castle, a clumsy effort having been made to paint over her initials on the trunk.

When confronted with this evidence Holmes denied having killed the Williams girls but he related a weird tale about Minnie attacking and killing her sister Annie, and to protect Minnie, whom he claimed to love, he advised her to go to Europe, and he carried Annie's body to the lake and sank it.

In 1880, I. L. Connor, a jeweler, married a beautiful eighteen-year-old girl named Smythe, in Davenport, Iowa. About one year afterward a little daughter was born. This child was named Gertrude. In 1889, Connor moved with his family to Chicago and he obtained employment in Holmes' drug store, which was located in the castle.

Mrs. Connor was still a beautiful woman, and being possessed of considerable business ability, Holmes consulted with her about several of his schemes, and they became quite confidential. Differences arose between Connor and his wife, with the result that he left, but Mrs. Connor and Gertrude remained at Holmes Castle.

In 1892, both Mrs. Connor and Gertrude disappeared. While in prison in Philadelphia, Holmes was interrogated as to their fate and he stated that Mrs. Connor died from an operation, but that he did not know what became of Gertrude.

On August 2, 1895, some of Mrs. Connor's wearing apparel was found in the castle and identified by her husband. On this same day janitor Pat. Quinlan and his wife confessed that they saw the dead body of Mrs. Connor in the castle. On July 22,

1895, A. Minier, a nephew of Mrs. Connor, swore to a warrant charging Holmes with her murder.

Her father, A. Smythe, produced a letter supposed to have been written by her in November 1892, wherein she stated that she contemplated going to St. Louis. Smythe stated that the writing was a poor imitation of his daughter's penmanship.

In 1892, Holmes was president of the A. B. C. Copying Company, which also had offices in the castle, and Miss Emily Cigrand was employed by him as a stenographer. She was formerly employed in a similar capacity at the hospital at Dwight, Ill., where Pitezel, under the name of Phelps, was being treated for a time. She was dismissed from this position and Pitezel recommended her to Holmes.

She and Holmes became very intimate and were known as Mr. and Mrs. Gordon where they had apartments near the corner of Ashland Avenue and West Madison Street. Miss Cigrand made a practice of writing several times a week to her parents, who resided in Oxford, Ind., but after December 6, 1892, they never heard from her again.

Holmes was suspected of having murdered several other persons with whom he had business dealings and who suddenly disappeared, but as the evidence against him in these cases is by no means conclusive, no details are given.

On July 28, Charles M. Chappell, of 100 Twenty-ninth Street, Chicago, reported to Lieutenant Thomas, of the Cottage Grove Station, that he worked for Holmes as a "handyman" during the summer of 1892. On October 1, Holmes asked him if he could mount a skeleton. Chappell said he thought he could, and Holmes gave him the skeleton of a man to mount, and when the work was completed Holmes paid him $36.

In January 1893, Chappell was given another skeleton of a man to mount. When Holmes first showed him the body, it was in the laboratory and there was considerable flesh on it. As Holmes had a set of surgical instruments and a tank filled with fluid for removing the flesh and apparently made no attempt to conceal anything from him, Chappell thought he was doing the work for some medical college.

In June 1893, Holmes gave Chappell another skeleton to mount, but as he never called for it, Chappell turned it over to the police on the day he made these disclosures.

On October 28, 1895, the trial of Holmes for the murder of Benjamin Pitezel began in Philadelphia. The work of selecting jurors had hardly begun when Holmes had a misunderstanding with his attorneys and they temporarily withdrew from the case. Holmes personally conducted the examination during their absence.

It was the theory of the prosecution that Holmes chloroformed Pitezel while the latter was either asleep or intoxicated. Three physicians testified that the death was caused by chloroform poisoning.

Mrs. Pitezel, who had become a physical wreck, identified a photograph as the picture of her deceased husband, and also identified the clothing removed from the body in the potter's field as having belonged to Mr. Pitezel. She then testified at length regarding the insurance swindle conspiracy and repeated the many conversations she had with Holmes regarding the whereabouts of her husband. To show that Pitezel was not contemplating suicide, as claimed by Holmes, Mrs. Pitezel produced a letter written by her husband some days previous to his demise, in which he expressed his intention to have his family join him in Philadelphia at an early date.

Several persons who knew Pitezel as "Perry" when he kept the place at 1316 Callowhill Street, identified the picture of Pitezel as the photograph of Perry. Many of them saw the corpse and stated that the remains were those of the man they knew as Perry. Several of these witnesses also testified that "Perry" was last seen alive at 10:30 P.M. on Saturday, September 1, 1894, when he visited a neighboring saloon to purchase a supply of whisky to last him over Sunday, the excise law preventing the sale of liquor on Sunday.

Eugene Smith, who placed the patent set-saw with Perry, testified to finding the body on the following Tuesday, and experts testified that the condition of the body indicated that the man was dead at least two days. This would mean that he died on Sunday.

Miss Yoke, who had believed she was Holmes' (or Howard's) legal wife, testified that she and Holmes were at this time living at 1905 North Eleventh Street. That on Saturday evening a man called to see Mr. Holmes, and that Holmes informed her that he was a prominent railroad man who was about to leave a large order for his patent copier, but that Holmes afterward admitted the man was Pitezel. She also stated that Holmes left their apartments at 10:30 A.M. Sunday and did not return until 4:30 P.M., at which time his excited and overheated condition attracted her attention.

They hurriedly packed their belongings and left that night for Indianapolis, remaining there but a few days and then proceeding to St. Louis, where Holmes called on Mrs. Pitezel. It was proved that on August 9, 1894, Holmes telegraphed $157.50 to the Chicago office of the Fidelity Mutual Life Association, to pay the half-yearly premium on Pitezel's policy. No witnesses were called for the defense.

In charging the jury, Judge Arnold, in commenting on Holmes' absolute power over Pitezel, said:

"Truth is stranger than fiction, and if Mrs. Pitezel's story is true, it is the most wonderful exhibition of the power of mind over mind I have ever seen, and stranger than any novel I ever read."

On November 2, 1895, the case was submitted to the jury, and after deliberating a short time a verdict of guilty was returned.

On May 7, 1896, Holmes was hanged in Moyamensing[3] prison, Philadelphia. He assumed an air of utter indifference to the end.

Some days before his death, when it was evident that all hope had vanished, Holmes made a "confession," wherein he admitted that he had killed twenty-seven persons, but on the scaffold he contradicted this statement and claimed that the only persons for whose death he was either directly or indirectly responsible, were two women upon whom he performed criminal operations.

---

3. 1835-1963, it was demolished in 1968

BENJAMIN PITEZEL

NO. 1316 CALLOWHILL ST., PHILADELPHIA, PA.
(WHERE HOLMES MURDERED B. F. PITEZEL)

ALICE PITEZEL

NELLIE PITEZEL

NO. 16 VINCENT ST. TORONTO, CANADA (WHERE HOLMES MURDERED ALICE AND NELLIE PITEZEL)

HOWARD PITEZEL

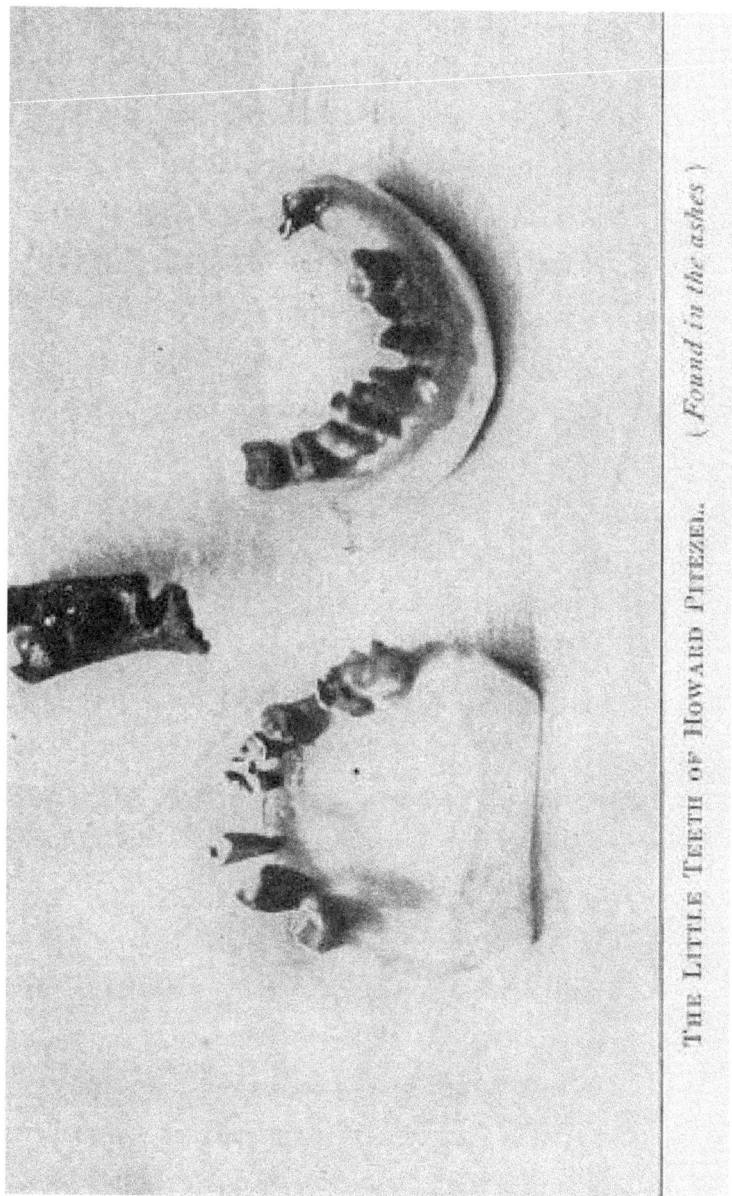

THE LITTLE TEETH OF HOWARD PITEZEL. (*Found in the ashes.*)

COTTAGE AT IRVINGTON, IND. (WHERE HOLMES MURDERED HOWARD)

NO. 26 WINOOSKI, AVENUE, BURLINGTON, VT.

(WHERE HOLMES INTENDED TO MURDER MRS. PITEZEL, DESSIE, AND THE BABY.)

THE CHICAGO TRIBUNE

SUNDAY, AUGUST 18, 1895

MODERN BLUEBEARD.

H. H. HOLMES CASTLE REVEALS HIS TRUE CHARACTER.

A New York paper reviews the case —
shows how the place made a veritable
factory for murders—a steel
chamber, a steel vault, a crematory,
 and quicklime graves— a dark shaft, a
trapdoor and a hanging cage among
the other furnishings.

NO CRIMINAL CASE OF RECENT YEARS has received more attention
from the public and the newspapers than that of H. H. Holmes.
Great papers have been devoted to it, and among the best reviews
of the case is the following from the New York World:

A veritable murder factory has been discovered in the house
built at Chicago by H. H. Holmes, who is charged with at least
eleven murders and suspected of many more. In this house built
and occupied by Holmes the police have found secret rooms without light or air, a sealed chamber, a hidden trap door leading to a
hanging secret room, and a steel bound-room built into the wall.

The second floor is a labyrinth of mazes, doors, and passages.

It contains a death shaft, where bodies could be lowered
into the cellar and from which a hidden passage led to the
sealed chamber.

One witness has already identified the room were Holmes
showed him three corpses on this floor of the house.

Another has described a narrow escape from death in one of
the dark rooms.

The cellar where large quantities of human remains have been
discovered, contains every provision for destroying bodies. Two
large vaults of quicklime, one of them containing some human
bones, have been found beneath the floor.

A hidden tank was found which contained a deadly oil, and
when this was unearthed an explosion followed which nearly cost
three of the workmen their lives.

Even more horrible than this was a discovery of a crematori-
um in the cellar where human bodies could be incinerated.

A woman's footprints discovered in a bed of quicklime in
the cellar is supposed to be that of Miss Williams, who was last

seen in this house and part of whose jewelry has been identified among the contents of a stove used by Holmes.

Human bones of all kinds have been dug up out of the cellar of this bluebeard[1]'s castle and the police have found tufts of hair, blood-stained linen, and pieces of clothing which has been hastily concealed.

These point not only to the commission of wholesale murder but led to the belief that many victims will yet be added to the long list of those whom Holmes is charged with killing.

He has already taken rank as the first criminal of the century, but the most astonishing thing about his career is the murder factory he erected in Chicago.

With all of this Holmes, whose real name is Mudgett, and who is imprisoned in Philadelphia, defies the police to convict him of murder, while admitting that he has been guilty of insurance swindling.

Holmes castle as it is called is an immense structure, with hundreds of rooms were victims could be "removed" with more expedition and safety than in the mountain stronghold of any feudal baron and of which none, but Holmes has ever known the secret. It was built immediately preceding the opening of the World's Fair, and there are many reasons to believe that Holmes, just then entering his murderous career upon a wholesale scale, contemplated gathering in victims among the visitors to Chicago.

There are hundreds of people who went to Chicago to see the fair and were never heard of again. The list of the "missing" when the fair closed was a long one, and in the greater number of foul play was suspected.

Did these visitors to the fair, strangers in Chicago, find their way to Holmes' castle in answer to delusive advertisement sent out by him never to return again? Did he erect his castle close to the fairgrounds so as to gather in these victims by wholesale, and, after robbing them, did he dispose of their bodies in his quicklime vats[2], in his mysterious oil tank with its death-dealing

---

1. A man who marries and kills each of his wives

2. A large tank or tube to hold liquids

liquids, or did he burn them in the elaborate retort with which the basement was provided?

These are questions that even the trial of Holmes may not answer, and which might even defy his famous namesake, "the Sherlock Holmes of Conan Doyle's creation." Certain it is that as the case progresses, increasing every day in dramatic interest other victims will be heard of who were last seen in the company of this fiend.

A LIST OF VICTIMS.

The list of his suspected murders thus far made up by those who are following the clues is a long one, and it is alone sufficient to give him easily first place in the century's category of crime. Here are the men, women, and children whom he is now believed to have made a way with:

-Conner, Julia L., divorced wife of I. L. Conner and bookkeeper for Holmes.

-Conner, Pearl, daughter of Mrs. Conner.

-Cigrand, Emeline G., daughter of Peter Cigrand of Anderson, Ind., stenographer for Holmes.

-Phelps, Robert E., who Holmes says married Miss Cigrand.

-Pitezel, Benjamin F., confidential agent and fellow-criminal of Holmes, killed in Philadelphia.

-Pitezel, Alice, daughter of B. F. Pitezel.

-Pitezel, Nellie, daughter of B. F. Pitezel, killed in Toronto.

-Pitezel, Howard, son of B. F. Pitezel, supposed to have been killed in Indianapolis or Detroit.

-Van Tassel, Emily, daughter of Mrs. M. L. Van Tassel of No. 641 North Robey Street, Chicago.

-Williams, Annie, of Fort Worth, Texas.; was visiting her sister when she disappeared.

-Williams, Minnie R., of Fort Worth, Tex., private secretary to Holmes.

Not all of these were murdered in the castle. Two of the Pitezel children met their end in a lone house in Toronto which Holmes had hired after their father had been killed in Philadelphia, as is now believed, by Holmes. This man appears to have been a victim of such a bloodthirsty and murderous disposition that he killed people here, there, and everywhere, and often without an apparent motive.

WHAT THE CASTLE IS LIKE.

But his castle, it now seems, as its labyrinths are explored, was his principal place of operation, and there it was that he planned and schemed and where many beautiful women are believed to have met their end. But such a place at his disposal, containing hundreds of rooms, torturous passages, secret chambers, trap-doors, dumbwaiters, with rope for lowering down bodies into vats, a tank and a retort for disposing of them, it is hard to understand why he went elsewhere to commit murders.

Holmes himself had planned the building, having no architect, and he took good care that the workmen were changed frequently so that no one should know what the interior of the structure was like. He had airtight chambers and a room of steel, lined with asbestos, where the wildest shrieks of his victims would be deadened, and he had a multitude of secret stairways and passages through which he could affect his escape at any time.

THE SECOND FLOOR.

The building which Holmes erected without paying out a cent for brick, stone, wood, or workmanship is a three-story brick, with stone basement foundation and wooden bay windows. These projections are covered with sheet iron.

The castle is 162 feet long and 50 feet wide, and from one end to the other is a labyrinth of narrow passages, twisting at all angles. In construction the basement and first floor are peculiar enough, but when the second floor is reached, the bewilderment is complete.

On this floor there are six halls. The most peculiar feature of the 35 rooms on this floor is the number and location of the doors. There are 51 of these doors. They are cut in the walls in every conceivable place.

Their location is such that no room, with the exception of the sealed chamber, is without an exit other than a door by which it might be entered. Some of the rooms have four doors, one opening on each side and each into a different room. By this means there are a dozen different ways of going from one end of the floor to the other.

The detectives say that it would be an absolute impossibility for a stranger in the building to catch a person familiar with the rooms, either in daylight or at night, for the doors are so numerous that any stranger would be confused in trying to pass the length of the building.

At the south end of the second floor is a space, which is neither hall nor room, through which a person can wonder several different ways on account of the irregular walls. In fact, there seems to be little else but walls in the area. On all sides except one, its only exits are through narrow passages, which two persons could not pass each other. This portion of the space, apparently, has been used for a kitchen, but the fire which Holmes is supposed to have started in the building two years ago have obliterated all traces of housekeeping.

THE SEALED CHAMBER.

Interest centers, however, around the mysterious small rooms in the middle of the floor. From two rooms which have access to the remainder of the floor you step into a dark closet. There are five doors leading into the closet, making it in reality only a framework for doors.

One of these doors opens into a good size closet. Another door opens into the sealed chamber. This door was boarded up when the search through the building first began, and it took an experienced eye to detect the presence of a doorway. When detectives Norton and Fitzpatrick, who had charge of the search for the supposed bodies of Minnie and Annie Williams, tore down the lathing and plaster they found themselves in a dark chamber, with no entrance save the one through which they had gone in.

This secret concealed chamber was one of the largest rooms

in the house. It is about twelve feet long and eight feet wide, it could not have been intended for a closet.

There was no furniture in it. The air was stifling when the detectives entered and there was no visible means of ventilation at that time. Later however, in a triangular end of the chamber, resembling a closet, there was found near the ceiling an opening which apparently ended in darkness.

Investigation showed that a shaft ran up a few feet and then, turning at a right angle, opened into the dummy elevator shaft. This shaft is large enough to admit the body of a man, and access to the sealed chamber could be gained easily by getting on top of the dummy elevator at the second floor and raising it a few feet.

THE SECRET TRAP DOOR.

The north door of the five opening into the closet, leads to the bathroom. In this room is a trapdoor in the floor, four feet long and two feet wide. Below it is narrow stairs which leads down into darkness.

After crawling down these stairs about eight feet, you stand in another secret chamber. This is situated about halfway between the first and the second floors.

This secret chamber is of about the size of the bathroom, seven feet by five feet but there's little floor space, on account of the stairs from above and a cut through which a second set of stairs descends.

At the south end of this secret chamber there is a door which is securely fastened. It is known however, to open on a stairway which leads down to the level of the first floor and communicates with a tin shop on Wallace Street. The tinner has built a bench against the floor. He says he knows that there is a stairway leading up, but he cannot tell where it ends.

THE DUMMY ELEVATOR.

The drug store has stairs leading down into the cellar and you can stand on these stairs and look up through the imperfectly built and burned plaster wall to the second stairway. The partition itself seems to be of no use except as a blind for the stairway. The dummy elevator shaft is about four feet square and formerly extended from below the third floor to the cellar. Lately it has been boarded up.

When Holmes erected this building, he said he was going to keep World's Fair "roomers" on the second floor. But most of his guests remained with him only a short time. He had his office on the third floor, in the northeast corner, and in passing from his drugstore to his office, he always passed through one or more of the rooms.

It was on this second floor that Holmes is supposed to have carried on most of his fine work. The janitor and his wife seldom visited this space, and most of the time Holmes had it all to himself. He had electrical devices which warned him as he sat in the drugstore when anybody walked over the floors of either the second or third story.

Minnie Williams, whom he is supposed to have murdered, oc-cupied a room just off his office. It is said that she was of a most jealous disposition and would get into a fury of passion whenever he was found in the company of other women. To protect himself from her espionage, he connected wires with a certain step on the stairway leading from the third to second floor, so that he was ap-prised immediately as soon as she either went down or up the stairs.

THE STEEL VAULT.

The steel-jacketed room was found on the third floor of the castle and next to the office used by Holmes. It is practically a bank vault.

In addition to a steel lining its sides are covered with asbes-tos to deaden sound. Its heavy steel door swings on a big pair of hinges.

Nobody but Holmes could open this safe, which was large enough for people to stand up and walk about inside. The lock on the door is an expensive one, and the whole structure was put into the building at a very heavy expense.

With the door once closed tight anybody inside would suffo-cate. A gas pipe, however, had also been introduced by Holmes, ostensibly to give light but in the opinion of the Chicago Police, to hasten the death of his victims. By blowing in any of the pipes on the outside he could extinguish the light in the locked steel room and the unhappy victim would soon be asphyxiated.

There was nothing in this steel room at the time of its discovery except some old papers, which were taken by the police. It is believed to be the only part of the murder apparatus on the third floor of the house.

On Friday of last week, the pick of a workman uncovered a strange device in the castle. In the room on the second floor where Holmes used to sleep a gas pipe runs over the floor. Where the pipe meets the wall, it turns down into the floor and beneath the boards is a cut off.

The pipe runs directly to the windowless room, where it is believed Mrs. Connor was murdered. The cutoff is believed to be one of Holmes' instruments of death. Sitting in his room he could turn on with ease a flow of gas that would fill the dark sleeping apartment and asphyxiate the occupants.

The cellar of the castle is, however, more interesting at present than the upper floors, because it is there the police have discovered remains of human bodies and the laboratory apparatus constructed by Holmes for making away with them.

It may be said right here that Holmes has all through the ramifications of his criminal career shown some shrewdness and foresight that even at the present moment there are serious doubts whether any one case of murder can be fastened upon him in a court of law. He covered up his tracks with a devilish ingenuity.

With all the forethought and caution of an educated man, familiar with detective methods and legal proceedings, he seems to have provided beforehand for every contingency [3]that might arise. Thus, in the case of the human bones dug up in the cellar of the castle, a game of astonishing shrewdness was unearthed.

When the officers searching in the cellar for evidence of crime had collected a godly number of bones, it was thought at last that Holmes' fate was sealed. Holmes, however, in his prison at Philadelphia, at once said that while the police officers were trying to fasten upon him every imaginable crime, an examina-

3. Unforseen event or circumstance

---

tion of this evidence would show that instead of being bones of human beings, they would be found to be soup bones which he had thrown on a refuse heap in the cellar.

Sure enough, an examination of these bones disclose the fact that some of them were soup bones, which could have no possible way be connected with murder. At the same time some of the others were discovered to be human bones, and the police at once saw that the soup bones had been purposely so place by Holmes to confuse possible searchers and break the force of any evidence, they might bring against him.

THE DEADLY OIL TANK.

It was July 20, when the police were hot in the investigation of the mysteries of the cellar of the castle, that the explosion occurred there which nearly cost some of the workmen their lives. Fire Marshal James Kenyon with two assistants was running a tunnel from the cellar towards the street, when they encountered a wall that gave forth a hollow sound.

As soon as this wall was broken through a horrible smell was encountered and fumes like those of a charnel house[4] rushed forth. A plumber was sent for and the workmen gathered about while he proceeded to investigate.

The first thing the plumber did light a match. Then there was a terrific explosion that shook the building, while the flames poured forth into the cellar. The plumber was the only man who escaped uninjured, and an ambulance took the other workmen to the hospital.

Then a thorough search of this mysterious chamber was made by the police. They found that the brick wall had concealed a tank curiously constructed. This tank had contained an oil whose fumes, the chemists say, would destroy human life within less than a minute.

WHAT THE OIL TANK DISCLOSED.

Holmes has given no explanation of the deadly oil found in his tank, but the history of the castle would seem to show that at one time he used the tank for ordinary swindling purposes. A small box was found in the center of his tank.

4. Building or vault where corpses or bone are piled

When this was opened by Fire Marshal Kenyon, an ill-smelling vapor rushed out. All ran except Kenyon, who was overpowered by the stench. He was dragged out and carried upstairs, and for two hours acted like one demented.

It was then discovered that the tank had at one time been connected with the gas main in the street. The swindler had organized the "Holmes Chemical Water Gas Company" with an alleged capital of $50,000 and had caught four men for an aggregate of $15,000. Holmes had filled the tank with water, had run a pipe with many jets up through the water, and had then turned on the gas from the main in the street.

Throwing in a handful of chemicals he then lit a match, and the gas had burned beautifully before the astonished eyes of his victims, who supposed that it was made from some new combination. The Englewood Gas Company finally discovered the leak, and Holmes was arrested for fraud, but was soon released. The connection with the main was then cut off.

A POTENT OIL.

This tank it has been pointed out, if filled with some corrosive acid, would destroy a human body, bones, buttons, clothing, teeth, and all in a few hours, so that not the slightest evidence of a murder would remain, and by pulling out the plug, the entire liquid would run down into the sewer. The oil found in the tank at the time it was discovered by the Chicago police would eat up human bodies in such a manner.

A CURIOUS FLUE[5].

The top of the furnace was two feet six inches above the top grate, just leaving room enough for a human body. It will thus be seeing that a brisk fire might have been kindled in this curiously constructed furnace, which was obviously neither for heating purposes nor for boiling water.

Then a human body might be placed upon the upper sliding grate and shoved in over the flames when the fire was hottest, to be consumed to ashes within a short time, leaving absolutely

5. Something that conveys heat

no trace. Clothing of all kinds might as easily be burned with the body.

A curious thing about this retort was that there was an iron flue leading from it to a tank. There was no other entrance to this tank. Was this to carry off the nauseous evaporations of consuming dead bodies? A white fluid was discovered in the bottom of the tank which gave forth an overpowering odor.

How many dead bodies of beautiful women, the victims of Holmes' passion and cupidity, have been burned in this retort? How many of the long list of "missing" visitors to the World's Fair have gone up in smoke in this fiery furnace and a cellar of the house where they had sought temporary lodging?

TWO QUICKLIME VATS.

But equally certain, if less speedy, as a means of concealing crime were the two tanks or vaults of quicklime discovered in the cellar of the castle. A body put into quicklime is eaten up and consumed in a short time.

Holmes knew this. He knew that this method of destroying bodies is followed by certain states with condemned criminals and that quicklime for such purposes has been in use from the earliest times. A druggist, such as Holmes pretended to be, would have no difficulty in buying all the quicklime he wanted, and it would naturally be stored in the cellar of his store.

These quicklime vaults discovered in the cellar of the castle were about the size of a grave and in one of them some bones were found. How many bodies have these quicklime vaults consumed? How many skulls, how many legs, how many arms have they eaten up and reduced to naught?

One tank found in the cellar of the castle was 14 by 16 feet in size. It was made of sheet-iron and was entirely covered by the cellar door. It had no apparent entrance. In the bottom of this tank were found some bones which are believed to be those of human beings.

BLOOD-STAINED LINENS

In an ash heap nearby were found pieces of linen that were blood stained. In another hole in the middle of the cellar more bones were found.

Elsewhere, under a heap of rubbish, the police came upon a letter written by Holmes to a druggist. In this letter was the following significant question:

"Do you ever see anything of the ghost of the Williams girls, and do they trouble you much more now?"

At one place in the cellar of the castle buried four feet under the surface, a pile of human bones was found. These have been examined by physicians, who declare that they include, among others, the bones of a child between six and eight years of age. There were seventeen ribs in all, part of a spinal column, a collar-bone, and a hip-bone.

It was while digging near this pile of bones that the police unearthed the two vaults of quicklime, and their proximity gave rise to a startling question. In spite of the retort, the deadly oil tank, and the two vaults of quicklime, all working at the same time, is it possible, it was asked, that Holmes was murdering people so fast that he had to bury some of them?

WHAT THE STOVE DISCLOSED.

Is it possible, the police have asked, that this man conducted murders upon such a wholesale scale that even the capacities of his well-equipped castle were outstripped and that he hurriedly buried bodies in the cellar, intending at some future time to throw them into the quicklime, the retort, or the deadly vat?

Even a stove which the police found in the castle seems to have been used by this fiend in furthering his ends. It was in this stove that the police found part of a gold watch chain which had been identified as having belonged to Miss Williams. The jeweler who sold it to her and twice repaired it for her says it is the same chain. Nearby was found a bunch of women's hair and women's shoes.

As to all these Holmes has given no reasonable explanation. He says the cellar contained gas generators, glass-melting, machines, and the like. But those who have examined the retort and the strange tanks say they could never have been used for such a purpose. He does not say how the human bones, partly consumed and unrelated, came into his cellar, further than to state that he dealt in human bodies, which he says he got from the cemeteries.

But he has been unable to give the name of a single individual who sold him such remains, nor has he told what cemeteries were robbed, or when. Even if bodies were stolen from graves, they would not contain pieces of jewelry.

Up to two weeks ago, when the Chicago police began to unravel the mysteries of the castle, there was probably no man alive, save Holmes, who knew of the existence of the sealed chamber, of the hidden trap door in the bathroom, and of the secret chambers, with the possible exception of Quinlan, the janitor. Quinlan has denied having any knowledge of the many mysteries of the building, and the Chicago police now believe that, no matter how intimate he may have been with Holmes or so much assistance he may have rendered and some of his crimes, nevertheless Holmes was too shrewd to take any one man completely into his confidence.

There is hardly a doubt that Pitezel knew of the secret rooms, passages, and chambers of the mysterious castle. He assisted Holmes in the erection of the building, and he slept there many times, but possibly he knew too much about it for the safety of Holmes, which may have been one of the reasons for his death in a lone house in Philadelphia.

Canada and Illinois are both trying to secure the extradition of Holmes from Pennsylvania, and the Governor of Arkansas has been asked to pardon a prisoner at Little Rock who offers to testify against him. Meanwhile, the collection of evidence against him goes on at the castle which is now Chicago's greatest curiosity.

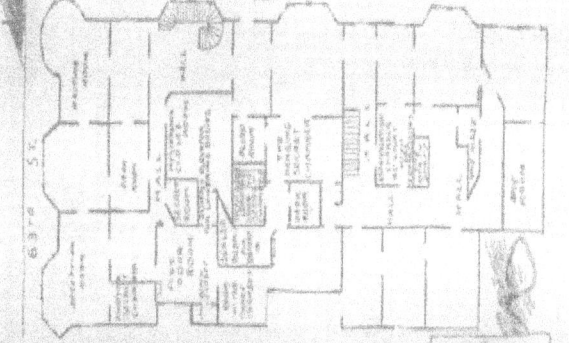

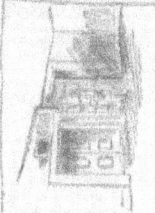

The Bloody Benders
(1872-1873)

THE BENDERS WERE A fake family made up of four people: John Bender Sr "Pa", Elvira[1] Bender "Ma" (it's unclear if she ever went by that name), their son John Bender Jr, and their daughter Kate Bender. They bludgeoned and slit the throats of travelers. When the townsfolk started investigating the murders, the Benders fled Kansas and were never caught.

In October 1870, two German immigrants arrived in southeastern Kansas, Pa and John Bender Jr. Pa spoke little English and he didn't speak much, he grunted. John spoke fluent English. Pa obtained 160 acres of land near the Osage Trail; the closest neighbor was three quarters of a mile away. Near the trail, the two built a one-room house that measured sixteen by twenty-four feet and had a nine-foot ceiling. The cabin was divided into two rooms by a canvas wagon-cover. The men lived in the smaller room in the back and turned the front into a general store and inn. Below the room there was a trapdoor leading to the cellar.

In the winter between 1870 and 1871, both Ma and Kate arrived. Ma, a relatively quiet woman, allegedly spoke very little English. Kate was reportedly flirtatious. She also claimed to be

1. Some sources call her Kate though it's not clear why

155

a gifted healer who said she could heal diseases and cure blindness and deafness.

During the spring of 1871, Labette County began experiencing many disappearances, particularly on the Osage Trail near the Benders' inn. In May 1871, a man named Jones was found dead in Drum Creek. His head was bashed, and his throat slit. During February in the following year, two males were found dead with their heads bashed and their throats slit. The Benders murdered six other people before a town-wide investigation started in 1873 when a well-known physician, Dr. William York, disappeared; his brothers, Colonel Edward and Senator Alexander York, brought the disappearance to public attention. The Bender's fled before the townsfolk discovered the body of York and many others when digging up the Bender's garden. It remains unclear why they murdered over eleven people. They were never seen in Kansas again. However, their true identities were later revealed. John Bender Sr., a man named John Flickinger and John Jr, a man named John Gebhardt. The only "truth" about the family was Ma, Almira Meik Griffith, and "Kate," Eliza Griffith, were mother and daughter.

For years people suspected two Michigan women to be Ma and Kate Bender. They had been apprehended but due to lack of evidence, they were released. Conflicting rumors about the Benders suggested they were killed, imprisoned, and living abroad. To this day, no one truly knows what became of the Benders.

TIMELINE

1870 -Tthe Benders move to Lavette County in Kansas

-Their cabin is built on the Osage Mission-Indepedence Trail

-The Benders open a small store in their cabin

1871 -In May, a body of a man named Jones is found in Drum Creek with his skull crushed and his throat slit

1872 -Two men are found with the same injuries as Jones

1873 -A well known physician, Dr. William York disappears

-York's disappearance sparks an investigation

-The township holds a meeting regarding the disappearances;

-Every homestead is searched

-A neighbor finds out the Benders are gone

- Volunteers dig up the garden and the rest of the Bender property

-York's body is found along with many others

The Kansas Chief

Thursday, May 22, 1873

The Devil's Kitchen!
Further Particulars of the Butcher Bender's Den.

[From The Kansas City Times]

THE FOUL AND DREADFUL SERIES of murders lately brought to light in Labette County, Kansas, continues to be the all-absorbing topic of speculation and conversation throughout the state, and to excite wonder and amazed horror all over the nation. Every item or circumstance connected with the horrid butchery is diligently sought after, and are made credulous by the fearfully true story of the damnable deeds of the Bender family, are made to drink in rumors and stories which have their foundation only in the imagination, which vainly labors to invent something more strange and horrid than the reality.

THE DEVIL'S KITCHEN,
Otherwise the Bender house is a small, rude frame shanty, without lath or plaster or intervening substance between its floor and the rafters of the pointed roof. In size it is 16x24 feet. Small uprights 2x4 inches are set to mark the house into two compartments, but no wall had ever been other than a white cotton cloth hung in the rear apartment and against these uprights. The front apartment had in a counter, over which the butchers once pretended to sell groceries. In the rear rooms was a bed, a table, a stove and three chairs.

The table, to which the guests of the fiends were seated, was placed directly over the trapdoor, so that the guest's back was to and against the white curtain. In this position it was an easy thing for the male villains in the front apartment to strike the form clearly lined and resting against the white cloth, and when the blows of the sledge and hammer had knocked the victim, with a crushed and broken skull, senseless and helpless to the floor, for the female fiends in the back room to cut their throat. The execution was as simple as it was dreadful, but, though it would seem resistance to such well-planned murder of the trusting and unsuspecting was impossible, the walls gave silent evidence that some of the murdered ones had not been sent to their doom without an effort to defend their lives. No less than a dozen bullet holes in the sides and roof of the house attest

that armed men, when struck down so relentlessly, had attempted to shoot their murderers, but, unfortunately, the aims had
been wild, and the murderers are reserved for the hempen halter.

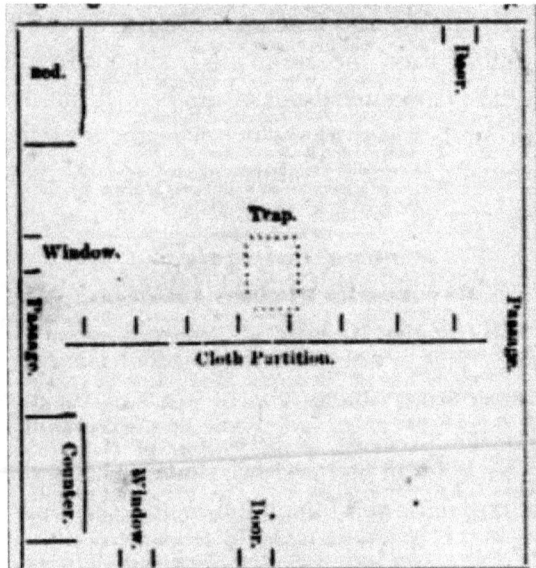

THE SITUATION.

The building is located just on the rising edge of a beautiful narrow valley, circled on south, east and west by a range of
mounds or hills, fronting to the north in the month of the valley.
The hills are distant from the house from a half mile to a mile,
the closest being on the south, to the rear. The house fronted to
the road just in the bead, sitting back about its own length from
the roadway. From this point of the road had a full view of everything for a half mile in every direction, but not another house is
within sight. It is about seven miles from Cherryvale, ten miles
from Thayer, eight from Ladore, and two from Morehead, and
just in the northwest corner of Labette County.

WHERE THE MURDERED NOW SLEEP.

With the exception of Dr. York and Henry F. McKenzie, G. W. Longeor and daughter, whose families took charge of their remains and buried them at Independence, the bodies of those found in the garden graves were quietly taken by silent men, who knew them not, yet longed for vengeance on their assassins, to the base of a high mound, about a mile to the southeast of the devil's kitchen, and there a second time returned to the earth to sleep until the final resurrection.

WHO THEY ARE.

The first of the eight bodies discovered was Dr. York, of Independence.

GEORGE W. LONGCOR AND DAUGHTER.

Mr. Longeor was a neighbor of Dr. York's, from whom he had purchased a team just before he started for Iowa, last December. He and his infant child were buried in one grave. He, as all the other men, had the back of the skull crushed in and broken and his throat cut, and the body stripped of nearly all its clothing. The child was placed at the father's feet, without a bruise or mark of violence, and with all its clothes on, even the hood and mittens, and many judge that the infant had been buried alive.

L. G. BROWN

was from Cedar Vale, Howard County. He had recently traded horses near Ladore and was supposed to have had about $60 with him. He was recognized by a silver ring on his finger, which was identified by the friend Johnson, with whom he had traded horses.

W.F. M'ROTTY

lived near Cedar Vale. He was en route to Independence to contest a land claim. One report says he had a large sum of money on his person, and another, judged to be more reliable, that he had but a small sum.

HENRY F. M'KENZIE

was from Hamilton County, Indiana, and was on his road to locate at Independence, where his sister, Mrs. J. Thompson, resides. He had but little money and was on foot and had been missing since December last.

PETER BOYLE

resided in Howard County. His body was so mutilated as to be hardly recognizable, but his poor widow identified him by his peculiar shirt, which her own hands had made for him. He had started on foot for Osage Mission sometime last December.

THE UNCONDEMNED.

The only one of the bodies not identified is supposed, and very reasonably, to be that of Jack Bogart, who started for Illinois, on horseback, about a year ago. The horse he rode has been found in the hands of a responsible man, who purchased him from one of the suspected confederates.

This completes the list of those yet discovered on the grounds.

PISTOLS AND KNIVES FOR SUPPER.

One of the most marvelous stories ever heard, but which is vouched for by reliable men, is the following: One evening about three months ago, a poor woman, footsore and weary, traveling to Independence, without money, stopped at the Bender den and asked for some supper and for privilege of resting a while. She was invited in, and being nearly exhausted, she took her shoes and wrappings off and laid down on the bed in the back room. She soon fell into a troubled doze, from which she was awakened by the touch of the old hag of the den who pointing to an array of pistols and double-edged knives, of various sizes, lying on the table, said in the spirit of hellish malignity[1]: "There, your supper is ready." The woman was motionless and breathless with terror, and as she sank back on the bed, the devil dame picked up the knives one by one and drew her finger along the sharpened blades at the same time glancing fiendishly at her intended victim. How

1. Causing harm, being dangerous and evil

long this terror lasted the woman could not tell, but at last she, in the very desperation of fear, arose as though not alarmed, and made a private, excuse for going out. She was permitted to do so, and moving around to the shelter of the stable, barefooted and scarce half clad, she darted off on the wings of fear, and ran for two miles to the house of one who protected her and gave her shelter. As she was running away, she turned frequently to see if she was being pursued, but no one followed her, though she saw the light from the open doorway several times, as though the devils inside were awaiting her return.

Even this story seems not to have aroused more than the before existing suspicion that the Benders were not exactly the right kind of people.

A BURGLING BUSINESS.

Although for the past three years this section has been infested with horse thieves and murderers, and this known to everyone about the thieves and murderers, and this known to everyone about the country, it is probable the same state of affairs might have continued for an indefinite period, had not the murder of Dr. York, a man of family, friends and reputation, led to the exposure. Men have been missed and bodies found of murdered men for three years past, and "vigilance committees" have hunted and driven some men from the country; but it would now seem as though the leaders of these "regulators" were themselves the villains, and honest men had been falsely and foully suspected and driven from their homes. Known villains have for that time been sent to the penitentiary, only to be pardoned out by governors.

And even the band of seventy-five armed and honest men who scoured the country in search of Dr. York, when it was learned he was missing, seem to have had very little judgment or discretion.

On the 28th of March last, Col. York[2] and Mr. Johnson visited the Bender house, to which place they had tracked Dr. York, and endeavored to coax some information from them, but they would tell nothing. On the 3rd of April this armed band visited the house with the sole object of finding the murderers of Dr.

2. Dr. York's brother

York, yet they did not notice the bullet holes in the house, and allowed themselves to be fooled by an assumed stupidity which was the disguise of most hellish cunning. The old hag sat mum and gloomy, pretending she could not understand or speak English; old Bender said nothing; Kate, she of the evil eye, denied all knowledge of the lost, and the younger male villain fooled them with a well made-up story. He said that at about the time they say Dr. York was missed, he, Bender,

HAD BEEN SHOT AT

in a lonesome place near Drum Creek, one evening, and it must have been by those who killed the doctor. He described the place minutely and then took them to it. And it was found as he said, and they half believed his story, and return with him. Col. York repeated the story given above, of the supper of pistols and knives offered to the lone woman, when the old hag soon found her sense of the English language improved, she understood all that had been said, and flew into a violent passion. She denied the story of the supper, and said that that was a bad and wicked woman, whom she would kill if ever she came near them again; that the woman was a witch and had bewitched Kate's coffee; and then she ordered the whole band away. While going and coming from the creek, John told Col. York that his sister Kate could do anything, that she could control the devil, and that the devil did her bidding. When they returned to the house, Col. York tried to induce this wonderful mistress of the devil to reveal where the body of his brother was. She positively refused her satanic aid at this time, giving a reason therefore that she could not do so in the day time, and while there were so many men and so much noise about.

AN INVITATION.

The pretended sorceress and real fiend then told Co. York privately that if he would come the next night, Friday — when best she worked her spells — and bring only one man with him, she would take him to the grave of his murdered brother. Had the Colonel been so foolish as to believe the mysterious power of the creature, there is no doubt she would have proved her promise good. The whole band then left the house. They visited the house of Roach and Smith and Harness, at Ladore and made many threats but accomplished nothing. Their intent was good, but they lacked an experienced detective for a leader. So strong was their conviction, however, of the guilt of the Roaches and of the Benders, that they would have hung them then had it not been for the persuasion of Col. York and a few others, who were determined that none but the known guilty should suffer. Of course this alarmed the Benders, and they fled.

MORE CARELESSNESS.

It seems strange that no watch was put upon the suspected Benders, and still stranger that they should have been gone three weeks before any knew of it. When they went to Thayer, they left their team and wagon and dog on the public street in the town. On the street the team and wagon remained for two days without a claimant, when they were taken charge of by a livery firm there — Bear & Wheeler. No notice, other than the item in the *Head Light*, the local journal, was given of the finding of the team, and no description of the horses published, though they were peculiarly and similarly marked. Had such description been given, it must have led to the speedy pursuit of the fleeing criminals. It is not suspected that there was any guilt in this neglect, but only carelessness.

THERE MUST BE A GANG.

No doubt is entertained that the Benders have not been alone in their damnable villainy. They must have had confederates to dispose of the stock and clothes of the murdered men, and suspicion has already pointed to a number of men, living throughout that section, in different directions, mid to none with more evidence of justice than one.

MIT. CHERRY.

This fellow lives about three miles south of Parsons, and when Col. York was making search for his brother, he tried to induce the Colonel to employ him as a detective. Luckily the Colonel would have nothing to do with him. This man, it is said by two men who are generally credited, at different places and times, and separately, told them that he was a member of a band of "Regulators" in the County, and that when they found a criminal, they never troubled him with the law, or put the County to any expense about him; that the band always knew their own work when they saw it, for every man they put out of the way they laid with his throat cut, his left arm across his breast, and his right by his side. In such condition were nearly all the Bender victims. As a further evidence against this fellow, it is known that soon after McCrotty's disappearance was known, and when there was about to be some action taken to look for him, he pretended to have a letter from McCrotty telling of his safe arrival in Illinois, at his intended destination.

The other suspected parties who have been arrested are men of bad repute in general, and believed for some time to be horse thieves, if nothing worse. On Sunday, Sheriff Stone brought into Independence, under arrest, Addison Roach, of Ladore, and Wm. Buxton, a son-in-law of the elder Roach, both found near Cedar Vale. This makes the number under arrest now on suspicion, so far was known, twelve.

LAST SUNDAY AT THE GRAVES.

On last Sunday there were about one thousand men, women and children, at the Bender grounds, gazing with mingled emotion of horror and curiosity. The graves ever yet sent forth a sickening stench and women held their noses as they peered down into the narrow tenantless boles. Two special trains were ran, one from Independence and one from Coffeyville, to a point on the railway line about two miles from the house, and teams were busy running to and from the cars to the grounds, while the greater portion of the crowd was compelled to walk. These trains brought about 600 persons. There were about six or seven hundred persons there from all parts of the surrounding county, in wagons, carriages, buggies, and on horseback.

The curiosity of many seemed to master their repulsion, and hundreds brought away some memento of the dreadful place. The blood-stained bedstead was smashed to pieces and divided in the crowd, all the shrubbery and young trees were broken or torn up and carried away, and pieces of the house, borne off by the curious. Such another raid would not leave much of the shanty. It was supposed that the grounds would be ploughed and scraped again this day to search for other bodies, but the intention was abandoned, and it is not probable any further search will be made until it is done regularly by the county authorities.

REWARD OFFERED.

Rewards to the amount of $5,000 have been offered for the capture of the murderers, and there is not the slightest doubt, but they will be recovered. On last Saturday the detectives were on the trail of the Benders, with the express certainty of effecting their speedy capture, and it is more than probable that they are already taken. With the number under arrest and the others watched, no doubt someone will reveal the whole truth, when Kansas will be rid of the worst scoundrels that ever infested and cursed this country.

*The Benders were never obtained and the true whereabouts of the Benders remained a mystery. To this day it is still unknown where the "family" had gone.

BIBLIOGRAPHY

Barclay, George L. "The Poison Fiend!." Internet Archive. N.p., 1872.

"The Devil's Kitchen!" *The Weekly Kansas Chief.* (Troy, Kan.) 1872-1918, May 22, 1873, Image 2". Chroniclingamerica. Loc.Gov, 1873.

Duke, Thomas S. *Celebrated Criminal Cases Of America.* Internet Archive. N.p., 1910.

Luscomb Haskell, E. "The Life Of Jesse Harding Pomeroy." Internet Archive. N.p., 1892.

"Modern Bluebeard. H. H. Holmes Castle Reveals His True Character." *The Chicago Tribune.* 1895, p. 40.

SUGGESTED READING

Becker, Ryan. *Murderous Minds Volume 1: Stories of Real Life Murderers That Escaped The Headlines.* 2018.

Garza, Phyllis De La. *Death For Dinner: The Benders of (Old) Kansas.* 2004.

Greig, Charlotte, and John Marlowe. *Serial Killers and Psychopaths.* 2017.

Keller, Robert. *The Deadly Dozen: America's 12 Worst Serial Killers.* 2014.

Larson, Erik. *The Devil in the White City.* Vintage Books, 2004.

Parker, RJ. *Cold Blooded Killers: School Shootings, Kids Who Kill, Mass Murders, Spree Killers.* 2014.

Rosewood, Jack, and Rebecca Lo. *The Big Book of Serial Killers: 150 Serial Killer Files of the World's Worst Murderers (Encyclopedia of Serial Killers).* 2017.

Schechter, Harold. *Deviant.* 1998.

www.ingramcontent.com/pod-product-compliance
Lightning Source LLC
Chambersburg PA
CBHW021927040426
42448CB00008B/945